What book of the Bible shall we study first? and What book shall we translate first? are two typical questions asked by new Bible study groups and by Bible-translating teams. In most cases the book chosen is the gospel of John. This is because John's gospel has a combination of many desirable features making it a primer for reading and study: it clearly presents foundational truths; it combines fact and interpretation; it presents the way of salvation succinctly and persuasively (e.g., 3:16); its very setting and atmosphere are universal; and it is picturesque and attractive in varied forms.

Introduction   Bible study can be one of your most enjoyable activities. Once you have tasted the thrill of personal, firsthand discovery, have sensed the illuminating help of the Holy Spirit in your study, and have seen how contemporary the Bible is, your approach to God's Word will take on a new dimension. It is the hope of this writer that this study guide will be an incentive for you to dig into the inexhaustible mine of God's riches as found in the gospel of John.

Suggestions for the home Bible class:

The many Bible classes which are meeting weekly in homes of our land are a bright indication of a healthy spiritual hunger of many for the bread of God's Word. The item common to these informal groups is the Bible. The classes are truly *Bible* classes if the Bible is the center of attention and discussion.

1

Below are given some suggestions and guidelines for making your Bible class a profitable one. Devote some time in the first meeting of your class to a discussion of these suggestions. In some cases, a suggestion may not apply to your class (such as the "refreshments" item).

The "ingredients" of a home Bible class:

1. *The Holy Bible and a study manual.* Use the same version, such as the King James, for the entire group, but have access to other versions for comparison of readings. A study manual used by each member of the class is a common basis for directed group study.

2. *The Holy Spirit.* The Holy Spirit is the unseen Miracle-worker in the class' pursuit of the goal. "Faith cometh by hearing, and hearing by the word of God" (Rom. 10:17). Depend on Him to make your class fruitful. (Read I Cor. 2.)

3. *The students.* If the group is hungry for the Word, the class will succeed. Christians will become stronger in their faith, and non-Christians will be stirred to think about accepting Christ as Saviour.

4. *The host.* The host is a key to atmosphere. New members or visitors should be invited by the host, not the leader.

5. *The leader.* The role of the leader is shepherd-teacher. A lay leader is to be preferred over a clergyman, because the home Bible class situation emphasizes the role of the laity. It should be noted here that a home Bible class is not intended to compete with the local church's Bible classes, but rather to supplement the program of the church. For example, many unsaved neighbors will attend a home Bible class who would otherwise stay away from a church. When they are saved, they will then recognize the need of entering into the fellowship of a local church where the gospel is faithfully preached.

6. *The fellowship.* The combination of students, host and leader should be a fellowship of common purpose. The group may be a mixture of Christians and non-Christians, but the common purpose of all is to learn what the Bible says and how it should be applied.

Suggestions for the students:

1. *Read.* Read every Bible verse cited in the manual, and study the manual carefully.

2. *Record.* Make notations in the margins of your Bible; record observations on paper; write out answers to questions in the manual.

3. *Inquire.* Don't hesitate to ask questions in the group meeting.

4. *Participate.* Share with others what *you* have learned in your study.

5. *Apply.* Be as obedient in applying the Bible to your life as you are hungry to know what it says.

Suggestions for the leader:

1. *Know the group.* Know the spiritual needs of the members of the class. Also, be aware of their knowledge of the Bible and study abilities.

2. *Be well organized.* Have the three parts of the meeting (opening minutes, main discussion, closing minutes) well planned, even though your plans are subject to extemporaneous adjustment in the course of the informal class meeting.

3. *Be well prepared.* In addition to studying carefully the Bible text and the manual's lesson, think of ways to use the charts of each lesson in the class meeting. The chart is an important visual aid and affords variety in group study.

4. *Ask questions.* Encourage the members of the class to participate. This is done most effectively by well-chosen questions directed to them. Also, never belittle any member's remarks or answers.

5. *Emphasize the main truths.* The leader should keep the class from wandering away from the main teachings of the Bible passage being studied. Watch for clues in the Bible text to such main teachings, or otherwise strong words and phrases. This study guide will be of help in this.

6. *Storm the will.* The hour of discussion should make a difference in the heart of everyone in the group. Persuade each one to examine the heart honestly, and to act accordingly.

7. *Further recommendations for the discussion hour.* Note: The size of the group should be kept relatively small. Start another group as the number increases.

   a. Open the meeting on time.

   b. Keep the entire meeting informal. It is not intended to be a formal worship service.

3

c. The opening minutes should be devoted to welcoming visitors, reviewing the previous group study, and identifying the goals of the present discussion.

d. Devote most of the hour to a free, informal discussion of the main parts of the lesson. Note: You may choose to devote more than one meeting to the discussion of any one lesson of this study guide. Illustrate the Bible passages from your own experience, and encourage the members of the group to do the same.

e. As you approach the end of the meeting, summarize the things learned, and let the members suggest ways to apply the Bible truths.

f. Make clear what the homework is for the next meeting.

g. Close the meeting on time. Light refreshments (if any) and further discussion (if sought) should be kept distinct from the stated class meeting hour.

Lesson 1

Background and Survey

FOUR MAIN STAGES ARE RECOMMENDED

FOR THE PERSON WHO WANTS TO STUDY

ANY ONE BOOK OF THE SCRIPTURES.

These stages are:
1. learning the *background* of the book (e.g., author, date written)
2. making a *survey* of the book as a whole
3. making a firsthand *analysis* of each part (e.g., chapter) of the book
4. referring to outside helps (e.g., commentaries) for supplementary and checking aid

This first lesson is devoted to the background of the gospel of John and a survey, or overview, of the book. The remainder of the manual is a guide to firsthand analysis of each chapter of John. The study suggestions and questions of those analytical lessons are of such a nature that you can complete each lesson without much, if any, reference to outside aids. (At times you will be directed to such aids for help on technical or problem passages.)

I. BACKGROUND.

A. Author.
Authors of many Bible books are not identified by name. This is so in the case of the gospel of John. The traditional view is that John the apostle, sometimes referred to as John the evangelist, was the author; hence the title, gospel of John, or gospel according to John.* (The titles of

---

* Another view is that a close disciple of the apostle, referred to as John the elder, was the book's author. See A.M. Hunter, *The Gospel According to John*, pp. 12-14.

our Bible books were not a part of the inspired text, but were added along the way for identification purposes.) According to 21:20, 23-24, the "disciple whom Jesus loved" was the author. Read 13:23; 19:26; 20:2; 21:7 for other similar descriptions of this disciple. In each case, John could be the disciple meant. If John was the author, why do you suppose he would not name himself in these passages?

Listed below are some descriptions and other facts concerning the Apostle John. Study these carefully to become acquainted with the author. Be sure to read all verses cited.

1. John was a son of Zebedee (21:2) and Salome (cf. Matt. 27:56; Mark 15:40; John 19:25). Since Salome was a sister of Jesus' mother Mary, Jesus and John were cousins. This would partly explain the close association between the two.

2. John was a brother of the Apostle James. Jesus surnamed both men as Boanerges, or "sons of thunder," a name indicating perhaps a fiery personality (cf. Luke 9:52-56).

3. Zebedee, James and John were fishermen at the Sea of Galilee. Zebedee was probably well-to-do (Mark 1:19-20).

4. John may have been a disciple of John the Baptist when Jesus called him to His service (Mark 1:20). His age at that time may have been around twenty-five, and he lived to be one hundred.

5. John was a Palestinian Jew, a close companion of Peter, and a contemporary of the events of his gospel.

6. John became a leader of the Jerusalem church (Gal. 2:9).

7. John wrote three epistles and Revelation in addition to his gospel. Because Revelation refers mainly to the last days, the comparison may be made that as John the Baptist prepared the way for the first coming of Jesus, the Apostle John prepared the way for His second coming.

8. There are only a few historical references to John after the events of the Gospels. Read these:

Acts 4:1-22 — John with Peter
8:14-15
Galatians 2:9 — One of John's contacts with Paul

Revelation 1:1, 4, 9 — John's exile experience,
around A.D. 95

9. From New Testament biography and epistles a composite personality image of John is seen, though incomplete in some respects. John was a man of courage, fervor, loyalty, spiritual perception, love and humility. The subject of love is a keynote of his epistles. Of this Merrill Tenney writes, "As Christ tamed his ardor and purified it of unrestrained violence, John became the apostle of love whose devotion was not excelled by that of any other writer of the New Testament."† (Cf. I John 4:7.)

A little may be learned about the man John from the book he wrote, although one is not usually aware of the author as his gospel is being studied. From that standpoint the authorship may rest in anonymity, suggested symbolically by someone's remark that "this gospel was written by the hand of an angel."

B. Date and Place of Composition.

The latter years of John's life were spent around Ephesus, hub city of Asia Minor, where the apostle was teaching, preaching and writing. The advanced nature of John's gospel points to the fact that the other three Gospels had already been written, and that a period of time had elapsed since their writing. Now the church's need was for a restatement of the same story of Christ, but with more reflection and interpretation combined with the narrative. On the basis of this it may be concluded that John wrote his gospel toward the end of the century, or around A.D. 85, while he was ministering at Ephesus.‡

Ten years later, around A.D. 95, John was exiled by Emperor Domitian to the island of Patmos, where he wrote the book of Revelation (cf. Rev. 1:9).

C. Original Readers.

By the time John wrote his gospel the church had matured in its transition from a Jewish exclusivism (cf. Acts 10) to a universal outreach. Hence it was very natural for this fourth gospel to be directed to a universal audience. This is why John translates Hebrew and Aramaic

† Merrill C. Tenney, *New Testament Survey*, p. 189.
‡ John's gospel is sometimes called "The Ephesian Gospel."

words (e.g., Siloam, 9:7; Gabbatha, 19:13; and Golgotha, 19:17), and why he explains Jewish religious practices (e.g., the burial custom of 19:40).

D. Style of Writing.

There is a basic simplicity about the language and structure of the fourth gospel, while the meaning of its message ranges from the perspicuous (e.g., 3:16) to the mystical (e.g., 1:1). Luther wrote, "Never in my life have I read a book written in simpler words than this, and yet the words are inexpressible." Another theologian has expressed it this way:

> The noble simplicity and the dim mystery of the narration, the tone of grief and longing, with the light of love shedding its tremulous beam on the whole—these impart to the Gospel of John a peculiar originality and charm, to which no parallel can be found.§

John is a book of contrasts, moving quickly from grief and sadness to joy and gladness; from the storms of opposition to the peace of fellowship; from condescension earthward to ascension heavenward; from doubt to faith; from life to death. Any attentive reader of this gospel must be stirred within as he ponders what its narrative has to do with him.

E. Purposes.

The three different writings of John (gospel, epistles, Apocalypse [Revelation]) reveal three different basic purposes of the author:

1. The gospel: the evangelic founding of the church
2. The epistles: the organic shaping of the church
3. The Apocalypse: the eternal future of the church ||

John explains specifically in 20:30-31 why his gospel was written. It was primarily to win *unbelievers* (Jew and Gentile) to a saving faith. John also must have had in mind the confirming of *believers* in their faith,# so that the church would have a stronger witness.

Read 20:30-31 for John's purpose in reporting the "signs" of Jesus in his gospel. The miracles were called "signs" by John because they *signified* vital spiritual truths. John

§ August Tholuck, quoted in John Peter Lange, *Lange's Commentary on the Holy Scriptures*, 17: vii.
|| *Ibid.*, p. 15.
The *New English Bible* translates 20:31 as "recorded in order that you may hold the faith that Jesus is the Christ, the Son of God."

8

wanted his readers not only to learn those spiritual truths, but to come to a personal relationship to Jesus through faith in Him as Christ, the Son of God. Keep in mind the words "believe" and "life" as key words of John's gospel. What is the connection between signs, belief and life?

John also had other purposes in mind, subordinate but related to those mentioned above. One was to refute the heresy of Docetism, which denied the true humanity of Jesus (observe John's "answer" in 1:14). Another was to expose the unbelief of Judaism** (e.g., "He came to his own country, but his own people did not receive him," 1:11, TEV).

THE SYNOPTICS AND JOHN

The Synoptics	John
chiefly concerned with Jesus' ministry in the north, around Galilee	gives more coverage to Jesus' ministry in the south, around Judea
much emphasis on "kingdom" inheritance	more emphasis on the person of Jesus ("I am's") and eternal-life inheritance
Jesus as Son of David, Son of man	Jesus especially as Son of God
the gospel of the infant church	the gospel of the maturing church
the earthly story	the heavenly meaning
Jesus' sayings generally short (e.g., parables)	more of the long discourses of Jesus
comparatively little commentary by the gospel writer	much commentary by John
only one mention of a Passover	three, possibly four, Passovers cited (on this basis it is concluded that Jesus' public ministry lasted 3½ years)

** The word "Jew" appears around seventy times in the gospel.

9

F. Relation to the Synoptic Gospels.††

The four canonical Gospels record an identical gospel ("good news") about the same God-Man, Jesus. Yet each gospel has its own unique function.‡‡ The one gospel markedly different from the other three is John's. Some of these differences are shown in Chart A.

Most of the comparisons shown on Chart A refer to the Gospels' contents *as a whole.* For instance, Jesus is no less Son of God in the synoptics than He is in John.

G. Coverage of Jesus' Life.

The four Gospels differ from each other as to how much they report of Jesus' life. Whatever each author included or excluded was determined by a divinely inspired selectivity with a view to the particular gospel's purpose.§§ After we have reconstructed from the four Gospels the main facts of Jesus' three and one-half years of public ministry, we can compare how much of that total ministry each gospel reports. Chart B shows the coverage of John's gospel, as indicated by the shaded areas.

1. Observe that John gives a full coverage of the first year of Jesus' ministry. What region of Palestine was mainly involved?

2. John also gives extensive coverage of the last months of Jesus' ministry. Like the other three Gospels, he gives special attention to Jesus' death and resurrection.

3. Read in your Bible the four references to Passovers cited on the chart. (Some hold that the "feast" of 5:1 was not of Passover time.)

4. Observe that one verse, 7:1, covers the entire six-month period of Jesus' specialized ministry. (The synoptic gospels give an extensive coverage to this period.) What would be the purpose of an author of a gospel, like John, to include in his narrative only certain events of Jesus' life?

---

†† The word "synoptic" is used to identify the similarity of Matthew, Mark and Luke. The word itself is from the Greek *synoptikos*, which means "to see the whole together."

‡‡ For a comparison of the four Gospels, see Irving L. Jensen, *Studies in the Life of Christ.*

§§ For example, Matthew omits Jesus' first miracle in Cana; Mark omits the nativity story; Luke omits Jesus' meeting with the Samaritan woman; John does not record Jesus' ascension to heaven. (Neither does John report Jesus' nativity and genealogy, youth, wilderness temptations, and transfiguration.)

THE LIFE OF JESUS   SHOWING COVERAGE BY JOHN (SHADED AREA)

Chart B

| PREPARATION | PUBLIC MINISTRY | SACRIFICE & VICTORY |

ASCENSION

40 days

2 months   RESURRECTION

DEATH

TRIUMPHAL ENTRY, 21:25

Matt. 21:1   John 11:55   12:12

OPPOSITION (INCREASING)

CONCLUDING MINISTRIES

3 months   PEREAN

BEYOND JORDAN, 10:40

John 10:40   10:22-39

3 months   LATER JUDEAN

TO FEAST OF TABERNACLES, 7:2—10:21

John 7:10

SPECIALIZED MINISTRY

THIRD YEAR

4 months   LATER GALILEAN   7:1

TO TYRE AND SIDON,

Matt. 15:21   John 6:4   chap. 6

EXTENDED MINISTRIES

POPULARITY (DECLINING)

10 months   MIDDLE GALILEAN   chap. 5

JESUS ORDAINS TWELVE, John 5:1

Luke 6:12 ff.

SECOND YEAR

4 months   EARLY GALILEAN

JESUS RETURNS TO GALILEE, 4:43-54

Mark 1:14   4:42

EARLY MINISTRIES

OBSCURITY (VANISHING)

8 months   EARLY JUDEAN

JESUS CLEANSES TEMPLE,

John 2:13 ff.   John 2:13

OPENING EVENTS

4 months

FIRST YEAR

JOHN INTRODUCES JESUS, 1:19

John 1:19 ff.

BIRTH   B.C.   ANNUAL PASSOVERS   John 1:1-18

11

II. SURVEY.|| ||

We have studied the background of the fourth gospel in order to appreciate more *how* and *why* it was given to the world. Now as we enter the stage of survey study, followed by analysis in the subsequent lessons, our goal is to learn *what* the gospel says and means.

Open your Bible to the gospel of John and rapidly turn the pages of its twenty-one chapters. As you do this prepare your mind to get a general overview of this book, just as one would view New York City from the top of the Empire State Building. This is what survey study is—seeing the structure of the book as a whole, and getting the "feel" of its contents. Survey study should always precede analysis. The rule is "Image the whole; then execute the parts." (Have you ever tried thumbing through a magazine first for a casual acquaintance, and then returning to read the individual articles and features?)

For your study you should use a Bible in which you will not hesitate to make pencil notations. Throughout your study, whether survey or analysis, always keep a pencil in hand as you read the Bible text, and use it to record your observations.

A. First Reading.

Your first reading of the gospel should be of a scanning type. Spend about an hour (averaging three minutes per chapter) viewing only some of the prominent features of each chapter.## Don't try to be exhaustive in this stage of your study. The main purpose of this scanning is to make a first acquaintance by identifying some of the book's contents. After you have scanned each chapter, record a chapter title on Chart C, similar to the titles shown. (Note: Divisions are made at 1:19, 10:40 and 12:36*b* instead of 2:1, 11:1 and 13:1, respectively.) Things to look for in this scanning are main characters (e.g., Lazarus, chap. 11), main events, and key words and phrases. You may choose to read only the first verse or two of each paragraph in a chapter, rather than all the verses of the chapter. (For

---

|| || For a detailed description of the survey method of study, see Irving L. Jensen, *Acts: An Inductive Study*, pp. 43-54.

Of course, the original Bible autographs did not have chapter divisions, or, for that matter, verse divisions. Such divisions are helps to us today for reference and for identification of small units of thought.

survey study, train your eyes to see things without tarrying over the details.)

What are some of your first impressions of John's gospel after this first reading?

B. Second Reading.

As you scan the gospel a second time, keep in mind the chapter titles you recorded earlier. Try to identify any turning points in the narrative, such as when Jesus becomes a prisoner. Try making a simple outline of the gospel, and record this.

Chart D is a completed survey chart showing various outlines which you will be referring to as you now use the following study suggestions:

1. Compare the first verse of John and the last verse._____

_____

2. How does 1:19 begin a new section? That is, how is 1:1-18 different from 1:19 ff.? _____

3. Generally speaking, to whom is Jesus extending His ministry in 1:19—12:36a? _____

Who are the special objects of His ministry in 12:36b—17:26? _____

4. What verses of chapter 5 show beginnings of opposition to Jesus? _____

JOHN: LIFE IN JESUS, THE SON OF GOD

Chart D

KEY VERSES:
20:30-31

OBJECT of BELIEF:
"Behold the Lamb of God"

DISCIPLES' BELIEF GROWING

GATHERING OF HIS OWN (6:35-51)

| CONFLICT WITH JEWS | MINISTERING TO HIS CLOSE DISCIPLES | CRUCIFIED BY HIS ENEMIES | RESURRECTION AND APPEARANCES TO HIS DISCIPLES |

PEOPLE'S UNBELIEF INTENSIFYING

KEY WORDS

believe (98)
world (78)
Jew (71)
Know (55)
glorify (42)
My Father (35)
verily, verily (25)
light, darkness
love
truth
abide, life
witness, testify
Word
judgment
name

Chapter references: 1:1 | 1:19 | 2:1 | 3 | 4 | 5 | 6 | 7 | 8 | 9 | 10:1 | 10:40 | 12:1 | 12:36b | 14 | 15 | 16 | 17 | 18 | 19 | 20 | 21

PROLOGUE

ERA OF INCARNATION BEGINS

YEARS OF CONFLICT

THE GREAT PAUSE

DAY OF PREPARATION
discourse and prayer

HOUR OF SACRIFICE
-cross-

DAWN OF VICTORY
-resurrection-

EPILOGUE

PUBLIC MINISTRY

PRIVATE MINISTRY

THREE YEARS

FEW DAYS

SIGNS WROUGHT
(MIRACLES)

SELF REVEALED
(DISCOURSES)

Chapter
● 2—Water to Wine
● 4—Nobleman's Son Cured
● 5—Sick Man Healed

Chapter
● 6—5,000 Fed
● 6—Walking on Sea
● 9—Blind Man Healed
● 11—Lazarus Raised

Chapter
14—The Father's House
15—Vine and the Branches
16—Promises of Jesus
17—High-priestly Prayer

Chapter
20—Resurrection
21—Postresurrection Appearances
● 21—Draught of Fishes

*—Four Passovers of John: 2:13; 5:1; 6:4; 11:55
●—Peculiar to John

Study the outline of Chart D concerning the people's unbelief, and compare this outline with the one shown of the disciples' belief. As you study John, keep in mind both of these developments.

5. The hour of 12:36b has been called "The Great Pause." How is this a turning point in the gospel? For help in answering this, identify the "they" of 12:37 and "his own" of 13:1. Then refer to Chart D and note the various outlines that have a turning point at 12:36b. _____

_____

6. In what chapter does Jesus' arrest take place? Where is the resurrection recorded? How are chapters 20—21 related to this resurrection? _____

_____

7. Do the verses 20:30-31 appear to conclude the main story of the gospel? If so, how do you account for the inclusion of chapter 21? _____
Observe that 21:24-25 has a reference to the *writing* of the fourth gospel, as does 20:30-31. Could you say that John has two endings? _____
Chart D shows chapter 21 as an epilogue. Compare this with the prologue of 1:1-18.

8. From Chart D, how long is the time period of 1:19—12:36a? _____
Compare this with the time period of the last half of the gospel. As was noted earlier, of the gospel writers only John reports Jesus' early Judean ministry, without which record Christ's ministry would seem to be only two and one-third years. To show how selective the gospel writers were, it may be noted that John reports events of only about twenty individual days of Jesus' public ministry. Read 21:25 for an explanation of the necessity of such selectivity.

9. Note the key words and phrases shown on Chart D. How many of these were key words which you had discovered earlier in your study? Each key word (e.g., "believe") suggests an important subject developed in John's gospel. Some time during the course of your study in John make topical studies of these. (An exhaustive con-

cordance, like Strong's, will identify all the verses in John containing such words.)

10. Note also by Chart D that 20:30-31 are given as key verses for this gospel. What are the key words of these verses? _____

Recall from earlier in the lesson the meaning of "signs." Observe on Chart D what chapters record the signs. Was Jesus' main purpose in performing the signs that of alleviating distress? How does 20:31 furnish an answer to this question? _____

11. The deity of Jesus is a main subject of John's gospel. Each chapter makes reference to this deity. Read the selected verses (one per chapter) shown below, and record the essence of each verse:

1:49

2:11

3:16

4:26

5:25

6:33

7:29

8:58

9:37

10:30

11:27

12:32

13:13

14:11

15:1

16:28

17:1

18:11

19:7

20:28

21:14

It will also be instructive to read personal recognitions of Jesus' deity, recorded in John, by these people:
John the Baptist (1:34)
Nathaniel (1:49)
Peter (6:69)
Martha (11:27)
Thomas (20:28)
John (20:31)
Christ*** (10:36)
From your study of the above verses, why is a belief in the deity of Jesus necessary for salvation?
12. Observe on Chart D the outline Signs Wrought; Self Revealed. Actually, in both main sections of John's gospel Christ was revealing who He was. In the last section, however, He pressed His claim more explicitly and revealed it fully in His death and resurrection.

Christ appears under many titles in this gospel, such as "the Word," "Creator," "Only Begotten of the Father," "Lamb of God." John records several "I am" testimonies of Jesus. Read those shown below, and record the identification made:

*** This is one of Jesus' own claims to deity. Only God Himself can rightfully claim deity. Since Jesus is God, He could make such a claim.

6:35

8:12

8:58 (cf. Exodus 3:14)

10:11

11:25

14:6

15:1

As you think about the above identifications which Jesus Himself made, list the many wonderful blessings and helps which are yours as a Christian because this same Jesus dwells within your heart.

Review Exercises

It is always good to review what has been studied in a lesson. See how many of the following exercises you can complete without referring back to the pages of the lesson.
1. What are the four main stages of studying any one book of the Bible? _____

_____

2. What do you know about John the apostle concerning these areas:
a. his family
b. occupation and religion before his calling to discipleship
c. relation to the early church
d. Bible books he wrote
e. his character
f. approximate age at death
3. When and where was the fourth gospel written? _____
4. Who were this gospel's original readers? _____
5. What is the main theme of this gospel? _____
6. Compare the fourth gospel with the synoptic gospels.

_____

7. What periods of Jesus' ministry are thoroughly reported by John? _____

_____

8. Name some key words of John. Quote the key verses. What title may be given this gospel? _____
9. See how much of the survey outline (Chart D) you can recall. Why is a new division made at 1:19; 10:40; and

12:36*b*? _____
10. How was "The Great Pause" a turning point in Jesus' public ministry? _____

_____

11. What is the general content of the prologue and epilogue? _____

_____

*   *   *

Your analysis of the text of John begins with the next lesson. Each lesson is divided into seven sections, described briefly below.

1. Introductory paragraphs. Here a main theme of the passage is identified, and continuity with the previous lesson established.

2. Preparation for study. This includes such suggestions as reading related Bible passages of other books, and setting up a work sheet for analysis.

3. Analysis. This is the heart of your own firsthand study. Spend most of your time here.

4. Notes. Some commentary notes and explanations are included here.

5. Further advanced study. This is for those desiring to do extra study related to the passage.

6. Some applications. It is always good to be reminded that Scripture was given to man *to be applied.* Then, the reminder calls for action.

7. Words to ponder. A key phrase or verse of the passage is quoted here, for a final meditation.

*   *   *

Here is a recommended list of study "tools" to be used for the exercises of this manual:

A Minimum List:

1. A good study Bible. Use an edition that has ample space in the margins for notations. Avoid using a small-print edition. (Note: Unless otherwise cited, the verses quoted in this manual are of the King James Version.)

2. Paper. Always have a sheet of paper or notebook handy for recording your observations and other notes.

3. Writing tools. A pencil, ball-point pen and some colored pencils are recommended for recording purposes.

Other Recommended Aids:

1. One or two modern versions of the New Testament, to compare readings of the passage being studied.

2. An exhaustive concordance (e.g., Strong's†††).

3. A commentary on John (a good one-volume commentary on the whole Bible, such as *The Wycliffe Bible Commentary*, is very adequate for these studies).

††† James Strong, *The Exhaustive Concordance of the Bible.*

ERA OF INCARNATION BEGINS   Prologue: "The Word Made Flesh"

WHILE THE WORLD WAITED AND WATCHED

VIA TELEVISION, ASTRONAUTS BORMAN,

ANDERS AND LOVELL CIRCUITED THE MOON.

They were on man's first lunar orbit. The voices of the astronauts added a unique dimension to the awesome flight in their reading of the Bible's record of the original creation—Genesis 1. "In the beginning God created the heaven and the earth."

Any thinking person is interested in the origin of the universe and of man. How did these come into being? The Genesis creation account gives the true answer—in the beginning of time God created the universe, including the highest creature, man.

The Apostle John knew and believed the Genesis creation story. The first three words of his gospel repeat the first three words of Genesis, and two verses later he makes the summary statement that all things were made by the "Word" (v. 3). From that point on, however, John's object in the prologue (1:1-18) is not to expand on the matchless cosmogeny of Genesis, but to show how this Creator Jesus was involved in His Father's plan of redemption for the fallen human race. This is the subject of our present lesson.

I.   PREPARATION FOR STUDY.

As you study each chapter in the gospel of John, keep in mind the general theme of the section where it is located. Chart D should be referred to for this. Chart E-1 is an excerpt from that chart.

21

1:1	1:19	2:1	3:1	4:1	4:54
PROLOGUE	ERA OF INCARNATION BEGINS				
OBJECT OF BELIEF Identifications of Jesus					

The section 1:1—4:54 seeks to show who Jesus is, as the object of man's belief. As you proceed in your analysis of 1:1-18, look for the ways Jesus is identified in these verses. Record your findings in the empty box shown. Continue this study for all the lessons devoted to this section.

II. ANALYSIS.

Segment to be analyzed: 1:1-18.
Paragraph divisions: at verses 1, 6, 14.
Your study of 1:1-18 should prove to be a stirring introduction to John's gospel if you open your heart and mind to the Spirit's voice. The passage is unexcelled in the Bible for its compactness of the gospel message. Examine each truth carefully. Weigh the significance of each fact, whether it is explicitly stated or implied. Learn all you can about Christ and His Father from these verses.

1. *Paragraph subjects.* Mark the paragraph divisions in your Bible. Always be paragraph-conscious as you study any one segment in the gospel. Since a paragraph is a group of verses with a common subject, you should try to determine what that subject is for each paragraph you are studying. Try this exercise for the three paragraphs of 1:1-18, and record your findings below.

1:1-5 :

1:6-13 :

1:14-18:

2. *Key words and phrases.* Read the passage again, with pencil in hand, underlining or circling repeated key words and phrases. Record these words and phrases on Chart F in the designated spaces, as often, and in the same order, as they appear in the Bible text. Some very important subjects are suggested by these key words, and are later developed by John in the gospel account that follows. If you are studying in a group, discuss these words as to meaning, significance, implications and applications.

3. *Topical studies.* Note the four topics shown on Chart F. Record on the chart all references to these subjects.

a. "The Word."

Does this phrase appear in the second paragraph? For the sake of effect, try reading verse 14 immediately after verse 1. Do you see any parallels in the phrases?

verse 1	verse 14
In the beginning was the Word, ——→	And the Word was made flesh
and the Word was with God, ——→	and dwelt among us
and the Word was God ——→	full of grace and truth

How do these verses make it clear that the "Word" must

be Jesus Christ? _____
Where in the prologue is Jesus Christ first identified by

name? _____
How does the title "Word" identify a main ministry of Jesus to this world? In answering this, consider the meaning of the phrase "he hath declared him" (1:18). The Greek word for "declared" as used in Acts 21:19 reveals

something of the main intent here. _____

Key Words and Phrases	TOPICAL STUDIES			
	"The Word"	The Human Race	Christ	Salvation

What is the normal function of words in everyday life?

Compare the three paragraphs using this outline:
  The Word in Creation (vv. 1-5)
  The Word in History (vv. 6-13)
  The Word in Incarnation (vv. 14-18)
Contemplate further this great miracle of Christ's incarnation, "the Word was made flesh." Compare Paul's comments on it as recorded in Philippians 2:5-11. Why

did Jesus unite with human flesh? _____

Did Jesus cease being God when He became a Man?

What is John the evangelist's answer to this? _____

Can you comprehend the doctrine of two natures (divine and human) residing in one person simultaneously? Does one's own inability to understand such a doctrine nullify its truth?
  Compare the words "grace and truth" (1:14) with the words "life" and "light" (1:4) These are good subjects for group discussion.
  b. The human race.
  Go through the entire segment and note all direct or indirect references to people. What is the predicament of

man suggested in the first paragraph? _____
In what sense is it true that Jesus "lighteth every man

that cometh into the world" (v. 9)? _____
What is meant by the phrases "the world knew him not" (v. 10) and "his own received him not" (v. 11)? (See

Notes on the phrase "his own.") _____

Who are the ones referred to by the first-person pronouns of these phrases: "*We* beheld his glory" (v. 14); "Of his

fulness have all *we* received" (v. 16)? _____
  c. Christ.
  We have already seen Christ referred to as the "Word."

25

What other titles or identifications are given Him? _____

_____

What aspects of His ministry are revealed in these identi-

fications? _____

Recall the content of the key verse 20:31. How does the prologue of John serve the purposes disclosed by that

verse? _____

_____

d. Salvation.

If the prologue of John were the only scripture teaching about salvation, how much could we learn? Consider these areas:

objects of salvation
need of salvation
character of salvation
prerequisite for salvation
transaction of salvation
life of salvation
Saviour of salvation
What is meant by the phrase "sons of God" (v. 13)?

_____

Who are sons of God now? _____

III. NOTES.

1. "Comprehended" (1:5). The word means "overcame."
2. Verse 11 may be read thus: "He came to his own country, but his own people did not receive him" (TEV). The first "own" is neuter; the second is masculine. "His own people" probably refers to Israel (cf. Matt. 23:37).
3. "Power" (1:12). The word means "authority."
4. "Grace for grace" (1:16). The intention of this phrase is that of one grace, or blessing, added to another as the believer appropriates each grace.

IV. FURTHER ADVANCED STUDIES.

1. You may want to learn more about this faithful servant of God, John the Baptist, who is given an honored place in the prologue by such brief references as "There was a man sent from God" (1:6). For such a study, read Luke 1:5-80; 3:1-6.

2. The Greek translated "dwelt" in verse 14 means literally "tabernacled." The Old Testament tabernacle was the place which symbolized God's *dwelling* with His people. Read Exodus 25:8-9, observing the word "dwell." With the help of a Bible dictionary or Bible encyclopedia make a study of the Old Testament tabernacle as a type of Jesus' ministry among men.

V. APPLICATIONS.

Anyone who reads the prologue of this gospel must acknowledge that it involves him personally. God and glory, men and darkness, Word and light, and a Christ that "dwelt among us" are words that suggest a redemptive movement from God to man which is to be found nowhere else in the world.

1. In what sense is Jesus God's Word to the world today?

_____

2. What light does Jesus offer all unsaved people? _____

3. What light does He offer to those whom He has given authority to become sons of God? Are you walking in

that light? _____

4. Are you appropriating the fullness of the life of Jesus in

you, enjoying blessing upon blessing from Him? _____

VI. WORDS TO PONDER.

"Out of the fulness of his grace he has blessed us all, giving us one blessing after another" (1:16, TEV).

Witnesses and Discoveries of Jesus

JESUS COULD NOT DO WHAT HE DID

UNLESS HE WAS THE PERSON HE WAS;

NOR WOULD PEOPLE FOLLOW HIM AS LORD.

So in the first days and weeks of Jesus' ministry His activities and contacts were such as would *introduce Him personally* to the world. The passage of this lesson records for us some of these major identifications made on Jesus' contacts with men at the beginning of His public ministry.*

I. PREPARATION FOR STUDY.

Read verses 1:6-8, 15, studied earlier, and recall that John here is identified as a *witness* of Jesus to men, that they might look to Him for salvation. The passage you are about to study gives more details of John's clear-cut witness of Jesus; how men found, or discovered, Jesus through that witness; and how they in turn became witnesses also.

You might want to prepare a work sheet similar to Chart G to record your observations in this study. Chart G shows a breakdown of the passage into three main units.

II. ANALYSIS.

Segment to be analyzed: 1:19-51.
Paragraph divisions: at verses 19, 29, 35, 43.
A discernible pattern throughout the passage is the repeated alternation between witness and discovery. The pattern is this: A witnesses to B; B discovers; B witnesses to C; etc. Follow this pattern for your analysis of this passage.

---

* Jesus' public ministry began officially on the occasion of His baptism, when from heaven came these words of ordination, "Thou art my beloved Son, in whom I am well pleased." (Read Mark 1:9-13.)

WITNESS	JOHN		JOHN AND TWO DISCIPLES	PHILIP AND NATHANIEL
	19	DISCOVERY	35	43
WITNESS	29	—		DISCOVERY
DISCOVERY		WITNESS		—
WITNESS	34	— DISCOVERY	42	WITNESS — DISCOVERY 51

1. John's Witness (1:19-28). Did John have a clear conviction of his mission? Read Isaiah 40:3 which John quoted (v. 23). _____ __

_____

2. John's Discovery (1:30-33). John the Baptist did not recognize Jesus when He came to John's baptism. But God gave John a sign of identification. What was it? (Cf.

Mark 1:10.) _____
3. John's Witness (1:29, 34). Contrast "This is he" (v. 30) with the earlier "Who art thou?" (v. 19). What were

John's two testimonies of Jesus? _____

_____

How does the one identify His humanity, and the other,

His deity? _____

The word Lamb suggests a slain lamb (cf. Isa. 53:7). What was the purpose of such animal sacrifices in the Old Testament? _____

Read Hebrews 9:22 and its surrounding context. Why did Jesus have to be God-Man to be an acceptable substitutionary sacrifice for the *sins of the world?* _____

_____

Observe how John witnessed to two of his disciples about Jesus (vv. 35-36).

4. The two disciples' discovery (1:37-40). How did these men first identify Jesus (v. 38)? _____

One day later they recognized Him as whom? _____

What brought about the discovery (v. 39)? _____

5. Andrew's witness (1:41-42a). How significant to a Jew is the statement "We have found the Messias"? _____

_____

6. Simon's discovery (1:42b). What is suggested by this verse as to what Simon discovered about Jesus? _____

_____

7. Jesus' witness (1:43). This is Jesus' witness concerning Himself. What do the words "Follow me" suggest about Him? _____

8. Philip's discovery (1:44-45). Who did Philip discover Jesus to be? _____

9. Philip's witness (1:45-46). What sound advice is contained in the words "Come and see"? _____

10. Nathaniel's discovery (1:47-51). What three titles did Nathaniel give Jesus (v. 49)? _____

What is the significance of this combination? _____

_____

11. Jesus' witness (1:50-51). What did Jesus reveal about Himself as to His relation to heaven and to earth? _____

_____

Compare the titles "Son of God" (v. 49) and "Son of man"
(v. 51). _____
12. One of Jesus' maxims was "Seek and ye shall find."
Discoveries come by searching. Review this passage and
observe the various kinds of searching which brought about
the various discoveries.
13. Continue the study begun in Lesson 2, where you
recorded on Chart E-1 identifications of whom Jesus was.
Record your findings on Chart E-2.

SECOND EXCERPT FROM CHART D

1:1	1:19	2:1	3:1	4:1	4:54
PROLOGUE	ERA OF INCARNATION BEGINS				
	OBJECT OF BELIEF				
The Word made flesh					
—Creator —True Man					

III. NOTES.

1. "Pharisees" (1:24). This "ultra" party of Jews claimed
salvation on the basis of physical descent from Abraham
and a strict adherence to the law. They rejected John the
Baptist because he preached that all people (Jew and
Gentile) were sinners needing to repent of their sins and
to look to Jesus as their Redeemer.
2. "John was baptizing" (1:28). This was not Christian
baptism, but a special temporary ordinance symbolizing the
washing away of sins. Thus John preached "the baptism of
repentance for the remission of sins" (Luke 3:3).

3. "Two of his [John's] disciples" (1:35). One is named Andrew (1:40). *The Wycliffe Bible Commentary* suggests the Apostle John as the other: "Silence regarding the name of the other points to the writer of the Gospel, who withholds his name out of modesty."†

4. "Messias" (1:41). For the benefit of his non-Jewish readers, John supplies the interpretation of this title: "the Christ." "Messias" is the Hebrew term for "the anointed one." The Greek word "Christ" comes from *chriō*, "to anoint." The Messiah or Christ was the One appointed and anointed by God to be the Saviour.

5. "Thou shalt be called Cephas" (1:42). When Jesus gave a surname to someone, the meaning of the new name suggested that particular characteristic of potentiality. "Cephas" was the Aramaic name for "Peter," meaning "stone." Peter eventually was to become a strong leader in the fellowship of the Christians (as the book of Acts bears out).

6. "No guile" (1:47). This commendation was not one of sinlessness, but of no deceit on the lips. That is, Nathanael was frank and honest. (Cf. I Peter 2:22; 3:10.)

7. "Son of man" (1:51). This was Jesus' favorite title for Himself, because it identified Him with the ones for whom He came to die.

IV. FURTHER ADVANCED STUDY.

1. The meaning and significance of Jesus' words become clearer to us when we are familiar with the various groups to whom He spoke. With the help of a Bible dictionary or encyclopedia, read about such groups as Pharisees, Sadducees, scribes, elders, priests, high priests, and Sanhedrin.

2. Study the subject of the Jews' Messianic hope in the days of Jesus. What kind of a king were they looking for, and on what Old Testament Scriptures did they base their

expectations? _____

---

† *The Wycliffe Bible Commentary*, p. 1075.

V. APPLICATIONS.

1. Many lessons about witnessing are taught in this passage. Make a list of these. _____

_____

2. What good traits of John the Baptist, revealed in this passage, should be coveted by Christians today? _____
3. In what sense do Christians have fellowship with Jesus today? What are the activities and blessings of such fellowship? _____

_____

4. Does God know and determine our potential for Christian living and service, and can He give the wisdom and power to fulfill His commission? _____

_____

5. Show evidences from contemporary history that assure you that Jesus is the exalted Son of God today (cf. Phil. 2:9). _____

_____

VI. WORDS TO PONDER.

"Thou shalt see greater things than these" (1:50).

The full Christian life is not a static experience, but a continuing relationship in which God reveals more and more of Himself to us, in the measure of our response to His revelation. The Lord is the Author of *great things*, and also of *greater things*. Is this our experience of Him?

Miracle Worker
and Voice of Authority

JOHN NOT ONLY RECORDED THE HISTORICAL

FACT OF JESUS' INCARNATION BUT GAVE

HIS PERSONAL TESTIMONY OF THAT GLORY.

John wrote in his prologue, "And the Word was made flesh, and dwelt among us, (and we beheld his glory, the glory as of the only begotten of the Father,)." Then John was moved to cite some of the first manifestations of Jesus' glory in signs which He performed before the public. Of the water-to-wine miracle, John writes, "This beginning of miracles did Jesus in Cana of Galilee, and *manifested forth his glory*" (2:11).

I. PREPARATION FOR STUDY.

1. Acquaint yourself with the geographical settings of this chapter. Locate on a map these places: Cana, Galilee, Nazareth, Capernaum, Jerusalem. Keep in mind the significances of the last four places, shown here:

Galilee—where Jesus performed most of His public ministry

Nazareth—where Jesus spent most of His life up to the time of His public ministry

Capernaum—Jesus' "headquarters" during His Galilean preaching tours

Jerusalem—the holy city; city of worship; with its temple, a symbol of God's meeting place with man; the city of Jesus' death and resurrection

2. The account of 2:13-25 is associated with the time of the Jews' Passover feast. Read Exodus 12:1-20 and Leviticus 23:1-8 to acquaint yourself with the background of this feast and its associate feast, the Feast of Unleavened Bread.

34

II. ANALYSIS.

Segment to be analyzed: 2:1-25.
Paragraph divisions: at verses 1, 12, 13, 23.
Mark the paragraph divisions in your Bible. Note on Chart H that the two short paragraphs are transitional ones.

JOHN 2:1-25

1 — 11	Transition verse 12	13 — 22	Transition verses 23-25

Read and reread the chapter, underlining in your Bible key words and phrases. Record on paper things that stand out in your mind after these readings. Record a paragraph title on Chart H for each of the two main paragraphs.

What do paragraphs 2:1-11 and 2:13-22 have in common as to what they teach about Jesus? _____

1. Read 2:1-11. What did Jesus mean by the first quoted words of verse 4 in light of the last phrase of His statement? _____

What was Jesus' relationship to His mother when He was a child and youth (cf. Luke 2:51)? _____

Compare also His tender relationship to her at His death (John 19:26-27). _____

On the phrase "mine hour" read these references to this in John: 7:30; 8:20; 12:23, 27; 13:1; 17:1. What was this hour? _____

Study the three words "miracles," "glory" and "believed" as they relate to each other in verse 11. Compare this verse with 20:30-31.

2. Read 2:12. What may have been the activities of these few days at the beginning of Jesus' public ministry? _____

What does the inclusion of such a verse in the gospel account contribute to the gospel's authenticity? _____

_____

3. Read 2:13-22. Compare this paragraph with 2:1-11. ____

_____

Compare your findings with these:

WATER TO WINE (2:1-11)	TEMPLE SCOURGING (2:13-22)
Home	Temple
Concern	Distress
Creation	Correction
Power and Glory	Authority and Life

In your group, discuss the meaning of each of the following terms: "passover," "my Father's house," "this temple." How are these terms related to each other? _____

_____

In what way was Jesus' coming resurrection a credential for doing what He did in the temple? _____

_____

Observe how Jesus was beginning to invite people to a position of faith in what He would do *in the future*, as well as in what He was doing at the time, in their presence. Make a list of all the things this paragraph teaches about Jesus. _____

_____

4. Read 2:23-25. How does the word "But" of verse 24 qualify the statement of verse 23? _____

_____

Compare 12:42-43. What is inferred by the statement "for he knew what was in man" (v. 25)? _____

_____

Relate this word "man" to the first four words of chapter 3. _____

What does this paragraph teach about the presence of Jesus; performance of Jesus; and knowledge of Jesus? ____

_____

5. Note how many times the name "Jesus" appears in this chapter. All other designations of Jesus are titles. The name "Jesus" comes from a Hebrew name meaning "Jehovah is salvation." Read Matthew 1:21 in this light. Also, what is meant by the phrase "many believed in his name" (John 2:23; cf. 1:12)? _____

6. How is Jesus identified in this chapter? Record your answers on Chart E-2, a project you have been working on for the last two lessons.

III. NOTES.

1. "They wanted wine" (2:3). That is, the supply of wine ran out. Wedding feasts in Jesus' day often lasted as long as a week.
2. "Woman" (2:4). This form of address was not one of disrespect (cf. 19:26), though Jesus' answer was one of refusal.
3. Two temple cleansings. Mark records a similar though different cleansing of the temple by Jesus (Mark 11:15-19). One was at the beginning of Jesus' ministry; the other at the end. The secularization and commercializing of the Jewish worship arena was religious corruption of the persistent kind. One might call it "Bedlam and Babble in the House of God."
4. "The Jews' passover" (2:13). The combined feast of Passover and Unleavened Bread was one of the three an-

nual feasts which all Jewish men were required to attend in Jerusalem (cf. Lev. 23:5-8; Exodus 23:17). Thus at Passover time the city was crowded with Jewish visitors from near and far.

5. Verse 17 in Today's English Version reads thus: "My devotion for your house, O God, burns in me like a fire."

6. "Forty and six years" (2:20). Herod's temple was begun around 20 B.C. and was completed in A.D. 63.

IV.   FURTHER ADVANCED STUDY.

Here are some subjects for further study:

1. Delve further into the study of strong words in the text, for example, "glory" (2:11). For outside help, a recommended volume on word-study is W. E. Vine, *An Expository Dictionary of New Testament Words*.

2. Make a study of all the Bible references to "wine."

3. Sometimes a symbolical meaning is suggested in the action of a Bible story, illustrating a biblical truth. Try to discover some symbolisms in the two stories of this lesson. For example, what is illustrated by the fact that water reserved for the Jews' religious rite of purifying was transformed into another product by Jesus?

V.   APPLICATIONS.

1. Examine your own heart and see if you can identify when your faith in Christ as Miracle-worker is the strongest. Is such a time associated with personal experiences, such as:

    a. when you are in special need
    b. when you are in a certain mood
    c. after you see a definite answer to prayer
    d. after prayer and Bible devotions?

How would you describe the *healthy* faith-life?

2. Is it possible for Bible-believing churches today to commercialize and secularize the activity of worship? Why is it so important that a spirit of worship should pervade a place of worship?

VI.   WORDS TO PONDER.

"He [Jesus] knew what was in man" (2:25).

Teacher Come from God

THUS FAR IN THE GOSPEL OF JOHN NOT

MANY ACTUAL SPOKEN WORDS OF JESUS

HAVE BEEN RECORDED BY THE AUTHOR.

A few commands of Jesus (e.g., "Come and see," 1:39; "Follow me," 1:43) and a few prophecies (e.g., "Thou shalt see greater things," 1:50; "In three days I will raise it up," 2:19) appear, but any extensive treatment on the subject of salvation is limited to the words of the gospel writer (e.g., 1:1-18) and of John the Baptist (e.g., 1:29-34).

Now in the design of his gospel, John breaks forth with the story of one of the greatest confrontations of Jesus with an unsaved man. The man was Nicodemus, an influential leader of the Jews. The subject of the conversation was the urgency and way of salvation. Nicodemus' informant was none other than the "teacher come from God."

Little did John know that one of the verses (3:16) of this passage would become a universal "golden text" of Christians in the centuries to follow.

I. PREPARATION FOR STUDY.

1. Relate this passage to what goes before. For example, observe "The Feats of Man" (2:20); "The Stuff of Man" (2:24-25); "The Desperate Need of Man" (3:3). What do you learn from reading the last phrase of chapter 2 and the first phrase of chapter 3 together, thus: "He knew what was in man. There was a man named Nicodemus"? Ponder afresh the tremendous truth that God is vitally interested in the spiritual condition of *each individual* person whom He brings into this world.

In relating chapter 3 to chapter 2, keep in mind also that Jesus had just challenged the system of Judaism.

2. Review the differences between the baptizing ministries of John the Baptist and Jesus. John called his ministry one of baptizing with *water* (1:31); that of Jesus he called a baptizing with the *Spirit* (1:33). Consider this as you study 3:5.

3. Review the story of Moses and the bronze serpent in Numbers 21:4-9. This is the Old Testament type referred to in John 3:14-15 (cf. 12:32-33).

4. Keep in mind the progressive study of identifications of Jesus which you began in earlier lessons. Recall John the Baptist's enthusiastic "Look, there is the Lamb of God!" (1:29). Search for new identifications in this chapter, and record them on Chart E-3.

THIRD EXCERPT FROM CHART D   Chart E-3

1:1	1:19	2:1	3:1	4:1	4:54
PROLOGUE	ERA OF INCARNATION BEGINS				
OBJECT OF BELIEF					
—The Word	Lamb of God —sacrifice	Miracle-Worker —power in nature			
	Son of God —true God				
—Creator	Messiah —Christ	Voice of Authority —authority in worship			
—True Man	King of Israel —King				

II. ANALYSIS.

Segment to be analyzed: 3:1-36.

Paragraph divisions: at verses 1, 16, 22, 31.

Read all of chapter 3 through prayerfully and carefully, with pencil in hand. Record key words and phrases of these paragraphs on Chart I.

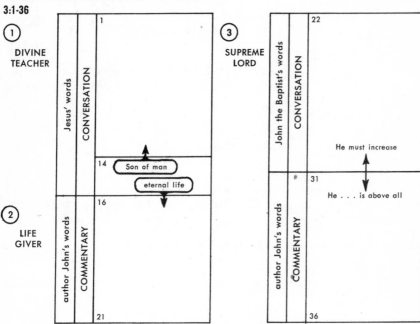

What is the theme of each paragraph?

The breakdown of paragraphs on Chart I is based on the interpretation that Jesus spoke the words through verse 15 (Conversation), followed by the gospel writer's words (vv. 16-21) (Commentary); and that John the Baptist's words appear in the next paragraph (vv. 22-30) (Conversation), followed by the gospel writer's words (vv. 31-36) (Commentary).*

A. Divine Teacher (3:1-13).

1. Who did Nicodemus recognize Jesus to be? _____

_____

2. How did Jesus demonstrate to Nicodemus that He was a unique Teacher, a divine Teacher? _____

* This commentarylike pattern of John's gospel distinguishes it from the synoptic gospels. Refer to commentaries for a discussion of possible interpretations as to where conversation ends and where commentary begins in this passage. Whoever is the source of the words in each case, of course, the teaching is divine truth.

41

3. What is the impact of the repeated phrase, "Verily,

verily, I say unto thee"? _____

4. What did Jesus deem necessary and vital to teach Nico-

demus? _____

5. Does the text say that Nicodemus asked for this teaching? On the basis of Jesus' words, what does it mean to be

"born again"? _____

B. Life-Giver (3:14-21).

1. Read 3:14-15. In the previous verses Nicodemus was
inquiring about the process of being born again (observe
the usage of "how" of vv. 4 and 9). Did Jesus explain the
process? In verse 14 Jesus reveals not the process but the

prerequisite for new birth. What is it? _____

_____

2. Compare Jesus' use of the word "must" in verses 7 and

14. _____

3. What elements of the gospel appear in 3:14-15? _____

_____

4. Observe Jesus' reference to Himself by the favorite
title of "Son of man" (3:14).

5. John does not record for us here what turn of heart
Nicodemus had as a result of his visit with Jesus. Read
7:45-52 and 10:39 for what is known about Nicodemus at
those later times.

6. Read 3:16-21. List the various truths about the gospel
taught by these verses. The word "saved" (v. 17) appears
two other times in John's gospel (read 5:34; 10:9). What

are the key words of John 3:16? _____

_____

_____

(Here is an interesting exercise: the first letters of what
words in 3:16 spell GOSPEL?)

C. Supreme Lord (3:22-36).

1. Read 3:22-30. What did John the Baptist mean by the words "He must increase, but I must decrease" (3:30)? Let the verses leading up to that statement give clues to your answer. _____

_____

2. Read 3:31-36. How do these verses give a basis for such a testimony as that of verse 30? _____

3. How is Christ here shown to be the supreme Lord? ____

_____

4. How is verse 36 a summary for the entire chapter? ____

_____

III. NOTES.

1. "Born of water and of the Spirit" (3:5). The reference to water may be symbolical of repentance and the spiritual cleansing coming from it, just as John the Baptist's water baptism was a baptism unto repentance (Matt. 3:11). Some interpret "water" as signifying cleansing by the Word (I Peter 1:23).

2. "Condemn" (3:17). The word is translated "judge" in some versions. The root meaning of the word is "separation." (Cf. "eternal judgment" of Heb. 6:2.) The eternal destiny of all unbelievers will be *separation from God*, not annihilation.

3. "The same baptizeth" (3:26). This refers not to actual baptizing by Jesus (cf. 4:2), but to the baptisms which His disciples performed *in His name* (and, perhaps, under His supervision).

IV. FURTHER ADVANCED STUDY.

Review the testimonies of Jesus by John the Baptist as recorded in chapter 1. Then observe the additional testimony recorded in chapter 3.

List all the comparisons and contrasts of this chapter, such as: flesh and spirit, earthly things and heavenly things.

V. APPLICATIONS.

1. What can be learned about personal evangelism from 3:1-15? _____

_____

2. Observe that Nicodemus was a learned "master of Israel," probably a member of the Jewish Sanhedrin (high court); and yet he was in darkness as to eternal truths. How do you explain that today there are many intellectual "giants" aware of what the Bible says who refuse to acknowledge its truth and pertinence? How can such people be reached with the gospel? _____

_____

3. What are some characteristics and expressions of humility in Christian living? What should the Lord have in your life: Place, Prominence, or Preeminence? _____

_____

VI. WORDS TO PONDER.

"He must become more important, while I become less important" (3:30, TEV).

"This Is Indeed the Christ"

WE HAVE ALREADY STUDIED THE FIRST OF

JESUS' MIRACLES IN CANA AND HIS

LENGTHY PERSONAL WITNESS TO NICODEMUS.

Chapter 4 of our present lesson deals with two similar ministries of Jesus: an extended personal witness to a woman of Samaria (4:7-42), and Jesus' second miracle, also performed in Cana (4:43-54). Before our study is concluded we will want to compare these two sets of similar ministries.

It is interesting to observe that although Jesus' ministries often involved the masses, such as preaching to large groups of people, more space is devoted in the Gospels to His dealings with individuals or small groups, such as families. The two stories of chapter 4 illustrate this. Jesus was ever conscious of *individual souls*. Surely all of God's servants today, living in a world whose streets are thronged with the masses, must constantly be reminded of their obligation to individual souls. Mass evangelism must move on and accelerate, but individual Christians must be faithful ministers to their neighbors.

I. PREPARATION FOR STUDY.

1. Recall that Jesus was in Judea as of the events of chapter 3 (cf. 2:13; 3:22). Now, at 4:3, "He left Judea, and departed again into Galilee." Look at the map (Chart T) and note that the direct route from the environs of Jerusalem to Galilee was through Samaria.

2. Keep in mind the origins and basic tenets of the religion of the Samaritans. Briefly, they are:

Origins: A small group of Jews was allowed to remain in Israel when the Assyrians took the northern kingdom captive in 722 B.C. These Jewish peasants intermarried with imported inhabitants from Assyria and other foreign lands, hence the beginning of a "half-breed" stock of Jews. Because of this stock admixture, Jews returning from Babylon to Jerusalem under Nehemiah around 445 B.C. refused the offer of Samaritans to help rebuild the holy city and its temple. Thus began a rivalry between the two peoples.

Tenets: Samaritans worshiped at their own temple on Mount Gerizim. They claimed their religion to be truly founded on the law of Moses. The Pentateuch (first five books of the Old Testament), with changes to conform to their beliefs, was their total Scripture.

II. ANALYSIS.

Segment to be analyzed: 4:1-54.
Paragraph divisions: at verses 1, 7, 16, 27, 31, 39, 43.
Read this chapter slowly and prayerfully. Make a note of all the important things taught about such subjects as everlasting life, true worship, the true Messiah, service to God, faith, and the purposes of miracles. The questions given below will direct you to these and other important quests.

A. Jesus and the Samaritan Woman (4:1-42).

1. SETTING (4:1-6).
a. What is implied in the statement "he must needs go through Samaria" (4:4)? _____

_____

What divine imperative of service is also suggested in these words? _____

_____

b. What does verse 6 teach about the humanity of Jesus?

_____

2. MEETING (4:7-26).
a. The prominent atmosphere of this passage is Jesus' personal concern for this Samaritan woman. What were the woman's needs? _____

_____

How did Jesus offer to help those needs? _____

---

b. What is said in this passage to support these statements:
For the castoff, there is contact.
For the unenlightened, there is teaching.
For the sinner, there is a way to God.
For the wistfully hopeful, there is hope fulfilled.
c. Jesus wanted people to know who He truly was. Observe how the woman identifies Jesus in these verses:

v. 9

v. 11

v. 19

v. 29

Observe that Jesus very clearly identified Himself as the Christ to the woman (v. 26). Complete your recording of identifications of Jesus which you began on Chart E-1. *d.* The woman was referring to Mount Gerizim when she said "this mountain" (v. 20). List all the things Jesus taught her about true worship in the verses that follow.

_____

_____

3. RESULTS (4:27-42).
Good results came of Jesus' encounter with the Samaritan woman. List these, paragraph by paragraph:

a. Concerning the woman (4:27-30) _____

_____

b. Concerning the disciples (4:31-38) _____

_____

c. Concerning the Samaritans (4:39-42) _____

_____

B. Jesus and the Nobleman's Son (4:43-54).

1. Relate verse 48 to the key verse of John, 20:31. _____

_____

2. Compare the man's "Come" (v. 49) and Jesus' "Go" (v. 50).

3. Observe how verse 50 records a *believing without seeing.*

How is this a test of genuine faith? _____

4. Observe the influence of the nobleman upon his whole house (v. 53).

III. NOTES.

1. Verse 9*b* is translated by Today's English Version: "For Jews will not use the same dishes that Samaritans use."

2. "Living water" (4:11). The woman did not comprehend what Jesus meant by living water in verse 10. She probably thought He meant the flowing, running water which is at the bottom of spring-fed wells.

3. "Salvation is of the Jews" (4:22). True revelation of God's salvation was to be found in Jewish institutions (e.g., the Old Testament Scriptures), not Samaritan. Jesus also may have been referring here to Himself, a Jew, as the Saviour.

4. "I know that Messias cometh" (4:25). The woman had some background of religious instruction. Passages such as Deuteronomy 18:15-18 of the Pentateuch taught the coming of an anointed Prophet.

IV. REVIEW OF 1:19—4:54.

Think back over the chapters of this first main section of John. You have been observing in your studies of these lessons the various identifications of who Jesus is. For this review, note different experiences of the following people in the presence of Jesus which brought about some measure of faith:

1. disciples at the wedding in Cana (2:11)
2. Jews at Jerusalem (2:23)
3. a ruler of the Jews (suggested by 7:45-52; 10:39)
4. Samaritan woman (4:29)
5. Samaritan townspeople (4:42)
6. nobleman and his household (4:53)

V. FURTHER ADVANCED STUDY.

1. Make a comparative study of the two Cana miracles (water to wine, 2:1-11; nobleman's son healed, 4:43-54) and the two conversations (with Nicodemus, 3:1-14; with the Samaritan woman, 4:7-42).
2. Many practical lessons on personal evangelism are taught in Jesus' encounter with the Samaritan woman. See how many of these you can derive from the passage.

VI. APPLICATIONS.

Let every Christian ask himself:
1. Am I aware of the personal need of strangers, with whom I come in contact, to hear the gospel and believe in Christ for salvation?
2. Do I consider some strangers to be outcasts, beyond my talking with them about their needs?
3. Am I honestly facing the fact that the spiritual "fields" of the world are waiting to be harvested?
4. Am I willing to be a sower, while another reaps?

VII. WORDS TO PONDER.

"We . . . *know* that this is *indeed* the Christ, the *Saviour of the world*" (4:42).

YEARS OF CONFLICT
Persecution Against Jesus Begins

AT CHAPTER 5 THE AUTHOR BEGINS TO

RECORD INSTANCES OF OPEN OPPOSITION

*TO JESUS BY THE JEWISH RULERS.**

A key phrase of chapter 5 is "For this reason the Jews began to persecute Jesus" (v. 16, TEV). Refer to the survey chart of John (Chart D) and observe that the section 5:1—12:36a is called "Years of Conflict." The chapters of this conflict section are widely selected stories covering a period of about two years. The climax of opposition comes in the hour of crucifixion, recorded by John in chapter 19.

Since we are beginning a new section in John's gospel, it is profitable to get another glimpse of the book as a whole. When studying a book of the Bible we don't want to lose sight of the "forest" as we walk among the many individual "trees." Chart J shows the four major sections of the gospel. Compare this outline with those of Chart D.

FOUR MAIN SECTIONS OF GOSPEL OF JOHN   Chart J

1:1	5:1	12:36b	18:1 21:25
IDENTIFICATIONS	CONFLICTS	PREPARATIONS	CRISES
— true — claims	— false — charges	— intimate — fellowship	— redemptive — work
INTRODUCTIONS TO THE PEOPLE	OPPOSITION BY THE JEWISH RULERS	INSTRUCTIONS FOR THE DISCIPLES	EXPERIENCES IN TRIUMPH

* In most instances in the Gospels, the word "Jews," in the context of opposition to Jesus, refers to the Jewish rulers.

As noted above, the conflicts with Jesus culminated in the crises of Jesus. In writing his gospel John chose to include a long section (12:36b—17:26) dealing with Jesus' intimate fellowship with His disciples just preceding His arrest and trial. The interrelationships of these four parts of John's gospel are shown in this diagram:

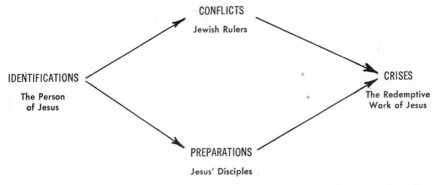

You will want to keep this survey in mind as you proceed in your study of the lessons that follow.

I. PREPARATION FOR STUDY.

1. Observe the time reference of this chapter, given in 5:1. This manual takes the position that the unnamed feast was a Passover feast.† (See Chart D for the other annual Passovers in John.) Thus one year transpired between the cleansing of the temple and the healing recorded in this chapter. Compare 2:13 and 5:1.

2. It may surprise you to see how incessant was the antagonism 'of the rulers and people against Jesus during these last two years of His public ministry. Even some of Jesus' disciples opposed Him on occasion. Read the following references, within the section 5:1—12:36a, and record your observations of the oppositions. An example is given.

As you conclude this study of opposition to Jesus, recall the prophecy written seven hundred years earlier by Isaiah, "He is despised and rejected of men" (Isa. 53:3).

† See A.T. Robertson, *A Harmony of the Gospels*, p. 42. Other views are that the feast was Tabernacles, Purim or Dedication.

Reference	Source of Opposition	Type of Opposition	Reason for Opposition
5:16			
5:18	Jews	sought to kill Jesus	Jesus claimed deity
5:43			
6:41			
6:52			
6:61, 66			
6:70			
7:1			
7:5			
7:11			
7:12			
7:20			
7:27, 30			
7:32			
7:41, 44			
7:45			
7:47			
8:6			
8:13			
8:48, 53, 59			
9:16			
9:22			
9:24			
10:19			
10:24, 31			
10:39			
11:46			
11:53			
11:56-57			
12:4			
12:10			
12:19			

II. ANALYSIS.

Segment to be analyzed: 5:1-47.
Paragraph divisions: at verses 1, 10, 17, 25, 30.
There are three main parts to chapter 5, shown by the outline below. Organize your studies around this outline.

The Beginning of Persecution.

1. DISCREDITING A MIRACLE (5:1-16).
a. What did the Jews' objection reveal about their sense of values? _____

b. Why was the time of the week not a deterrent to Jesus' miracle-working? _____

2. DENYING DIVINE AUTHORITY (5:17-29).
a. What authority for miracle-working did Jesus claim?
_____

b. How intimate was this Father-Son relationship? _____
3. REJECTING THE WITNESSES (5:30-47).
a. List the various witnesses which Jesus cited as proof that
He was doing the work of God. _____

b. How were the people rejecting those witnesses? _____
_____

III. NOTES.

1. Verse 39 may be read thus: "You study the Scriptures because you think that in them you will find eternal life. And they themselves speak about me!" (TEV).
2. "He [Moses] wrote of me" (5:46). Of this Lange's Commentary writes:

> Moses wrote of Christ, as the seed of the woman that shall bruise the serpent's head (Gen. 3), as the seed of Abraham by which all the nations of the earth shall be blessed (Gen. 12ff.), as the Shiloh unto whom shall be the gathering of the people (Gen. 49),

as the Star out of Jacob, and the Sceptre that shall rise out of Israel (Num. 24:17), as the Great Prophet whom God will raise up, and unto whom the Jews should hearken (Deut. 18). Moreover, the moral law of Moses, by revealing the holy will of God and setting up a standard of human righteousness in conformity with that will, awakens a knowledge of sin and guilt (Rom. 3:20; 7:7), and thus serves as a school-master to bring us to Christ (Gal. 3:24). Finally, the ritual law and all the ceremonies of Mosaic worship were typical of the Christian dispensation (Col. 2:17), as the healing serpent in the wilderness pointed to Christ on the cross (Num. 21:9; John 3:14).‡

IV. FURTHER ADVANCED STUDY.

Study this chapter for all the evidences it furnishes concerning the deity of Jesus Christ. How is Jesus God by being Son of God?

V. SOME APPLICATIONS.

This chapter is a severe rebuke to formal, legalistic religion and to unbelief. Just as Jesus healed the man who had been crippled for thirty-eight years, He can take a soul dedicated to a dead cause and transform it to newness of life. Why are there so many lifeless religions in the world today? What have you learned in this chapter about belief and unbelief?

VI. WORDS TO PONDER.

"Sir, I have no man . . . to put me into the pool" (5:7).

‡ John Peter Lange, *Lange's Commentary on the Holy Scriptures*, 17: 197–98.

Bread of Life Refused

JESUS WAS REJECTED BY THE JEWS

AT JERUSALEM BECAUSE OF WHAT HE

DID AND WHO HE SAID HE WAS.

This was the story of chapter 5, which we studied in the last lesson. Now we learn from chapter 6 that Jesus was also rejected at Galilee, not only by Jewish rulers, but by followers who were even beginning to call themselves His disciples.

There is a year interlude between chapter 5 and 6. (Compare 5:1 and 6:4.) The synoptic gospels record various events that transpired during that time. The purposes of John's gospel did not require the inclusion of these in the account.

I. PREPARATION FOR STUDY.

This is a long chapter, and it would be well to see its structure as a whole before analyzing its parts. Chart K shows this structure.

Make a survey reading of the chapter with this outline in mind, observing how the paragraphs are related to each other. For example, how did the miracle of feeding (6:1-15) bring on the discourses (6:22-59)? Also, what two paragraphs involve only Jesus and the twelve disciples?

II. ANALYSIS.

Segment to be analyzed: 6:1-71.
Paragraph divisions: at verses 1, 16, 22, 25, 35, 41, 52, 60, 67.

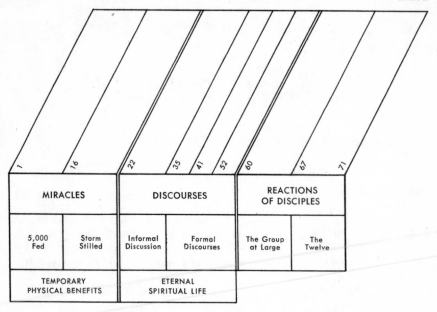

MIRACLES		DISCOURSES		REACTIONS OF DISCIPLES	
5,000 Fed	Storm Stilled	Informal Discussion	Formal Discourses	The Group at Large	The Twelve
TEMPORARY PHYSICAL BENEFITS		ETERNAL SPIRITUAL LIFE			

A. Miracles (6:1-21).

1. Compare the two miracles as to setting and need; power demonstrated; methods used; and effects. _____

_____

_____

2. What kind of king did the people want to make Jesus, according to verse 15? _____

3. Why did Jesus want to be alone at this time? _____

_____

B. Discourses (6:22-59).

1. Why were the people hunting for Jesus (v. 26)? _____
2. What is the basic difference between seeing a miracle and eating miraculous bread (v. 26)? _____

3. Center your study about Jesus' key testimony: "I am the bread of life" (v. 35). Make a list of all the things Jesus taught relating to His being this bread from heaven.

What did the people mean when they said to Jesus, "Lord, evermore give us this bread" (v. 34; cf. v. 36)? _____

C. Reactions of Disciples (6:60-71).

(Note: The disciples of verses 60-66 were the large group of followers, not the select group of twelve. This is clear from the distinction made in 6:67a and by the word "many" in verses 60 and 66. The disciples of verses 3, 16, 22 and 24 were the twelve.)

1. What was the stumbling block for many of Jesus' followers at this time (6:60-66)? _____

2. Compare the testimony of Simon Peter, in verse 69, with the key verse of John, 20:31. _____

III. NOTES.

1. The miracle of the feeding of the five thousand is the only miracle common to all four Gospels.

2. A denarius ("pennyworth," 6:7) was the average daily wage of a laborer in Jesus' day.

3. "Eat the flesh of the Son of man, and drink his blood" (6:53). Jesus was no doubt anticipating the Last Supper (Luke 22:14-23) when He spoke these words.

IV. FURTHER ADVANCED STUDY.

1. Go back over this chapter and observe how Jesus' disciples were receiving training in discipleship. A suggested path of inquiry:

a. in fellowship with Jesus (6:1-4)
b. in impotency (6:5-9)
c. in service (6:10-13)
d. in solitude (6:14-15)
e. in commitment (6:67)

2. Refer to commentaries for help in explaining the membership of Judas, "a devil," in the chosen circle of the twelve.

V. SOME APPLICATIONS.

1. Do you believe God can still perform miracles? Do you pray believing He can do "impossible things"?

2. Do you sense Jesus' nearness in experiences of fear? Do you hear His "It is I; be not afraid"?

3. Are you appropriating all there is of Jesus as you live the Christian life?

VI. WORDS TO PONDER.

"Will ye also go away?" (6:67).

Attempts to Arrest Jesus

JESUS IS THE ONLY MAN WHO HAS FULLY

KNOWN AND OBEYED THE WILL OF THE

FATHER CONCERNING HIS LIFE ON EARTH.

Jesus knew why He was sent to this world, what He must say and do, when and how His hour of death would come, and where He would go after death. He knew when He should hide from the multitudes, and when He should appear before them publicly. And He also knew that the time and manner of His death did not depend on his hiding nor on His public exposure, but on the predetermined appointment of His heavenly Father.

When Jesus healed the impotent man in Jerusalem, the Jewish rulers sought to kill Him (5:18). Jesus returned to Galilee to fulfill a ministry there relatively unhindered (6:1—7:1). When the Feast of Tabernacles (October, A.D. 29) was at hand, Jesus' hour of death was only six months away (Passover, April, A.D. 30). Since His Father had some ministries for Him to fulfill around Judea and Perea before His death, it was the right time for Jesus to go to Jerusalem during this holiday, even though there would be constant attempts at His life from then on.

Your study of chapter 7 will reveal how Jesus remained untouched though He walked into the mouth of the lion of the enemy at Jerusalem. The two most prominent truths of this chapter are:

1. Jesus' clear consciousness of His mission and His hour
   "I am from him, and he hath sent me" (7:29).
   "My time is not yet full come" (7:8).

2. The enemies' failure to seize Jesus
   "No man laid hands on him" (7:30).

I. PREPARATION FOR STUDY.

1. Refer back to Chart B to see what part of Jesus' public ministry is covered by the passage of this lesson (7:1-53). Chart L is an excerpt from that chart.

EXCERPT FROM CHART B   Chart L

Extended Ministries		Specialized Ministry	Concluding Ministries	
4 months	10 months	6 months	3 months	3 months
EARLY GALILEAN	MIDDLE GALILEAN	LATER GALILEAN	LATER JUDEAN	PEREAN
4:43-54	chap. 5 · chap. 6	7:1	7:2—10:21	10:22-39 · 10:40 ff.
SECOND YEAR		THIRD YEAR		

PASSOVER (6:4)   PASSOVER (11:55)

Observe that the six-month Later Galilean Period is passed over by John with the brief mention of 7:1. Our detailed information concerning Jesus' ministry at this time is furnished by the synoptic gospels.

2. The action of 7:2-53 took place in October, during the Feast of Tabernacles (7:2). Observe the progression in Jesus' relationship to this feast as you compare these verses: 8, 10, 14. Read Leviticus 23:34-44 and Deuteronomy 16:16-17 for descriptions of this popular Jewish festival which marked the conclusion of the harvest season.

II. ANALYSIS.

Segment to be analyzed: 7:1-53.
Paragraph divisions: See tabulation below.

Study the chapter to see the various types of opposition against Jesus, and the clear-cut testimonies which Jesus gave concerning His mission on earth. Concerning the latter, note the repetitions of the phrase "he that sent me." Record your observations on paper, following this format:

Paragraph	Opposition by Jewish rulers ("Jews")	Opposition by the people	People who defended Jesus	Teachings of Jesus
1-9				
10-13				
14-24				
25-31				
32-36				
37-39				
40-44				
45-53				

Make a note of anything you do not understand, and discuss such questions in your group.

III. NOTES.

1. "As the scripture hath said" (7:38). Jesus here does not quote any particular Old Testament verse, but gives the essence of various passages which describe miraculous waters proceeding from God. Some such passages are Exodus 17:6; Isaiah 44:3-4; 58:11; Ezekiel 47:1-9; Joel 2:23; and Zechariah 14:8.
2. "Doth our law judge" (7:51). See Deuteronomy 1:16.

IV. FURTHER ADVANCED STUDY.

1. Study the various questions of this passage. Compare the people's questions with those of Jesus.
2. What does this chapter teach about the Jews' expectation of the Messiah ("Christ")?

V. SOME APPLICATIONS.

1. How strong and sure is your sense of mission for Christ today? Can you say, as Jesus did, "He that sent me . . ."?
2. Are "rivers of living water" pouring out from your heart today, as a result of the Spirit's ministry? And are those rivers a source of blessing to others?
3. Are you quick to judge people before you listen to their case? (Cf. 7:51.)

VI. WORDS TO PONDER.

"And every man went unto his own house" (7:53).

The verse is deeper than it appears. It singles out individual hearts, individual homes. It doesn't say how many were believers or unbelievers. Truly it is a sobering conclusion to the chapter, suggested in the following outline:

Reactions to Jesus
Officers' Reaction: AWE
Nicodemus' Reaction: JUSTICE
Pharisees' Reaction: SCORN
People's Reaction: MIXED

Light of the World Rejected

CHAPTERS 8—9 CONTINUE DESCRIBING THE

JEWS' GROWING ANTAGONISM AGAINST JESUS

DURING THE FEAST OF TABERNACLES.

His enemies sought to kill Him, but no man could lay his hands on Him, because the time of His sacrifice had not yet come. He had more things to teach them before He would let them take Him.

 * The subject of sin—forgiven sin and unforgiven sin— is prominent in these two chapters. It is interesting to observe that Jesus does not introduce the subject. People (scribes and Pharisees in 8:3, and His disciples in 9:2) approach Him with questions about sin, and He responds with the truth. To sinners walking in darkness Jesus declared, "I am the light of the world" (8:12).* Some of His hearers believed; but for the majority, He was the *rejected light.*

I. PREPARATION FOR STUDY.

The best preparation for studying this lesson is a review of the previous lesson. Observe the continuity of thought and tone from chapter 7 to chapter 8. Also, compare these two verses:

"And every man went unto his own house" (7:53).

"Jesus went unto the mount of Olives" (8:1).

II. ANALYSIS.

Segments to be analyzed: 8:1-59 and 9:1-41.

Paragraph divisions: See Chart M.

Chart M is a survey of 8:1—9:41 centered about the sub-

 ° Read I John 1:5-9 for the connection between sin and the picture of darkness.

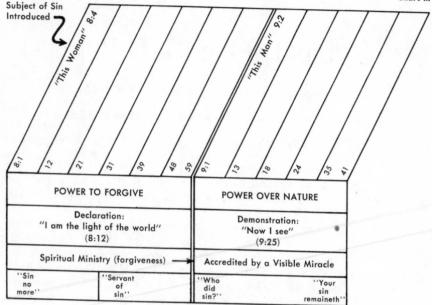

Subject of Sin Introduced

"This Woman" 8:4

"This Man" 9:2

8:1 | 12 | 21 | 31 | 39 | 48 | 59 | 9:1 | 13 | 18 | 24 | 35 | 41

POWER TO FORGIVE	POWER OVER NATURE
Declaration: "I am the light of the world" (8:12)	Demonstration: "Now I see" (9:25)
Spiritual Ministry (forgiveness) →	Accredited by a Visible Miracle

| "Sin no more" | "Servant of sin" | "Who did sin?" | "Your sin remaineth" |

ject of forgiveness of sins.† Note the various two-part outlines of this chart. How is chapter 9 related to chapter 8?
Read in your Bible 8:12 and 9:5, observing how the statement "I am the light of the world" connects the two chapters.

1. First, read each paragraph and record a paragraph title
on the chart.

2. Compare the opening events of each chapter (e.g., "this
woman," 8:4; "this man," 9:2). How is the subject of sin
introduced in each case?

3. Study the context of the phrases about sin shown on the
chart:

"Sin no more" (8:11).
"Servant of sin" (8:34).
"Who did sin?" (9:2).
"Your sin remaineth" (9:41).

† Most New Testament authorities, on the basis of manuscript evidence,
conclude that 7:53—8:11 was not written by John, though a record of true
fact. It cannot be demonstrated, however, that this paragraph, regardless of
authorship, was not inspired as the rest of Scripture and intended of God to
be included in John's gospel at this point.

4. Read the paragraphs again and note any reference (stated or implied) to forgiveness. Include in this topical study any fruit of forgiveness, such as "ye shall be free indeed" (8:36). Did the healed man of chapter 9 eventually experience forgiveness of sins?
5. Make a list of what is taught in these chapters about
    a. opposition to Jesus
    b. claims of Jesus
    c. truths of the gospel message

III. NOTES.

1. "Now Moses in the law commanded us" (8:5). This was a reference to Leviticus 20:10; Deuteronomy 22:23-24.
2. "Thou art a Samaritan" (8:48). As noted in an earlier lesson, a Samaritan was of mixed stock (Jewish and foreign), claiming to be of the only true religion descended from Abraham. The base intent of the charge against Jesus is obvious.

IV. FURTHER ADVANCED STUDY.

In these chapters Jesus says more about His Father. Make a study of this subject as it is taught throughout the entire gospel of John.

V. APPLICATIONS.

1. Do you have the forgiving spirit exemplified by Jesus in this passage?
2. Are you a "disciple indeed," continuing to live in the Word of Christ (8:31)?
3. How does truth make a man free (8:32)? How does Jesus, the truth, make a man free (8:36)?
4. You believe in Christ; do you worship Him (9:38)?

VI. WORDS TO PONDER.

"The night cometh, when no man can work" (9:4).

The Good Shepherd Spurned

JESUS WAS DISTRESSED WHEN HE HEARD

THAT THE JEWISH RULERS HAD CAST OUT

THE BLIND MAN WHOM HE HAD HEALED.

Like a shepherd recovering a lost sheep, Jesus found the man and brought him into His flock, in vital spiritual relationship to Himself (9:35-38). This event was the occasion for Jesus telling the multitudes the beautiful parable of the good shepherd, which is the main subject of our present lesson.

I. PREPARATION FOR STUDY.

This passage is of two parts, separated in time by about two months. This is shown by Chart N. (Compare Chart B.)

FEASTS OF TABERNACLES AND DEDICATION   Chart N

October: Feast of Tabernacles (7:2)		December: Feast of Dedication (10:22)	
7:2—9:41	10:1	10:22	10:39
Beginning of the Later Judean Ministry		Close of the Later Judean Ministry	

LUKE
10—13
RECORDS EVENTS
HERE

Read 7:2 and 10:22 for the two time references. Then note how the two parts (10:1-21 and 10:22-39) are brought together by the common subject of shepherd (e.g., "The sheep hear his voice," 10:3; "My sheep hear my voice," 10:27).

II. ANALYSIS.

Segment to be analyzed: 10:1-39.
Paragraph divisions: at verses 1, 7, 19, 22, 31.
The parable of the shepherd is one of the most beautiful of Jesus' picture stories about Himself.* You will want to tarry long over this passage to gather its many wonderful truths. Record your observations below.

Elements of the Parable (10:1-6)	Jesus' Interpretations and Applications (10:7-18)

* The Greek word of 10:6 translated "parable" is not the usual word so translated in the Gospels, but the literary form of the discourse is basically the same.

Who of Jesus' day (e.g., in chap. 9) were thieves, robbers and hirelings? _____

_____

Who would they be today? _____
What is meant by each of the following statements:
"I am the door of the sheep" (10:7) _____

"He shall be saved, and shall go in and out, and find pasture" (10:9) _____

"That they might have life . . . more abundantly" (10:10)

"They shall never perish, neither shall any man pluck them out of my hand" (10:28) _____

What reason did the Jews give for threatening to stone Jesus (10:33)? _____
Observe that they wanted to distinguish between His words and His works. How did Jesus relate His words and works (10:38)? Compare 20:31. _____

_____

What miracle was wrought in 10:39? _____

III. NOTES.

1. "Shall go in and out" (10:9). This is a familiar Old Testament expression for the activity of a leader (cf. I Sam. 18:16; II Sam. 3:25). The picture is a composite of freedom, safety and sustenance.
2. "Other sheep I have" (10:16). Since Jesus is speaking primarily to Jews, the reference to *other* sheep probably means Gentiles.
3. "Ye are gods" (10:34). The quote is from Psalm 82:6, where the reference is to judges. The same Hebrew word is translated "judges" in Exodus 21:6.

IV. FURTHER ADVANCED STUDY.

Make a comparative study of the shepherd psalm (Ps. 23) and this shepherd parable.

V. APPLICATIONS.

Write a list of all the blessings you as a believer can claim because Jesus is your Shepherd.

VI. WORDS TO PONDER.

"The sheep follow him: for they know his voice" (10:4).

The King of Israel Enters Jerusalem

THE HOUR OF JESUS' DEATH WAS FAST

APPROACHING, AND HE WAS WELL AWARE

OF WHAT HINGED UPON THAT DEATH.

Not once in His ministry did He panic or despair. Every event purposefully pointed to the cross, so that His constant testimony was, "For this cause came I unto this hour" (12:27). In this lesson we will be studying some of the key experiences of Jesus which took place at the close of the period of open conflict with the religious rulers.

I. PREPARATION FOR STUDY.

Chart O gives a survey of the events of the passage of this lesson. Study this before you begin to analyze the various parts of the passage.

FINAL MINISTRIES AND ENTRY INTO JERUSALEM   Chart O

10:40	11:1	11:45	12:1	12:12	12:20 12:36a	
PEREA	BETHANY	TO ·EPHRAIM	BETHANY	\multicolumn{2}{c}{ENTRY INTO JERUSALEM}	Jesus "did hide himself from them" (12:36b)
		①	②			
	Lazarus Story →	Two Sequels		The King comes (12:13)	The hour is come (12:23)	
\multicolumn{4}{c}{Final Ministries in Perea and Vicinity}	\multicolumn{2}{c}{Final Entry into Jerusalem}	The Great Pause

The name Lazarus appears in the story even after the section 11:1-44. Read these references and observe the connections: 12:1, 2, 9, 10, 17.

II. ANALYSIS.

Segments to be analyzed: 10:40—12:11; also 12:12-36*a*. *Paragraph divisions*: at verses 10:40; 11:1, 5, 17, 28, 38, 45, 54, 55; 12:1, 9; also 12:12, 20, 27.

As you analyze the two segments of this passage, follow the outline shown below. It may help you to record this outline in the margins of your Bible, to give direction as you read the text.

A. Final Ministries in Perea.*

1. PEREAN MINISTRY (general description, 10:40-42). What references to John the Baptist are made here? What does this teach about the fruits of faithful witness? _____

_____

2. AN INTERRUPTION OF THE PEREAN MINISTRY (11:1-44). What is taught in this story of the raising of Lazarus at Bethany, about:

the will of God _____

walking in spiritual light _____

resurrection life _____

faith _____

Jesus' compassion _____

the power of Jesus _____
3. TWO SEQUELS OF THE LAZARUS MIRACLE.
a. Counsel against Jesus by the Jewish rulers (11:45-57).

What was the rulers' fear? _____

  * The name Perea does not appear in the Bible. It refers to regions on the eastern side of the Jordan opposite Judea and Samaria. "Beyond the Jordan" (*peran tou Iordanou*) is Perea.

71

How did Caiaphas reason that Jesus' death would save the

nation of Israel? _____

Observe from 11:53 that at this point there was an organized plot to take Jesus' life. What did this cause Jesus

to do (v. 54)? _____

Does this indicate that Jesus had more work to do? Let the last phrase of 11:54, "There [he] continued with his disciples," be a clue as to the kind of work Jesus wanted to do before His death.

b. Supper in Bethany, Lazarus attending (12:1-11).

Lazarus' presence spoke of resurrection. What did the ointment symbolize (see v. 7)? Both Caiaphas and Mary unwittingly were prophesying the redemptive sacrifice of Jesus. But compare the hearts of Caiaphas and Mary. Also compare the hearts of Judas and Mary.

B. Final Entry into Jerusalem.

Once the opposition against Jesus came out into the open in the early part of His ministry, it never waned. Over and over again the Apostle John has had to record how Jesus was despised and rejected of men. It must have lightened John's heart to pen the triumphant account of the triumphal entry into Jerusalem of Jesus as He was lauded by multitudes as "the King of Israel."† The march itself was prophetic; when John wrote about it the prospect of kingship was assured.

Jesus' march into Jerusalem took place on Sunday, the first of the six days of Passion Week (Sunday through Friday). On Friday Jesus would be hanging on the cross.

1. PEOPLE'S ACCLAIM (12:12-18).

Why were so many people paying homage to Jesus

(12:17-18)? _____

Recall from your reading of the last few chapters that many people were believing on Jesus (e.g., 10:42; 11:45; 12:11).

---

† Of course when John penned these words a half century after the event, he recalled that many of the people lauding Jesus in the march were soon mocking Him on the cross, a change wrought about because the people's expectation of a Messianic inauguration at this time did not come about.

2. PHARISEES' DESPERATION (12:19).
Who comprised most of Jesus' enemies: the laity, or the
religious rulers? _____

_____

What influence do false religions have on the world today?

_____

Can the true church of God prevail? (Cf. Matt. 16:18.)

_____

3. GREEKS' QUEST (12:20-22).
Ponder the significance of the words, "Sir, we would see
Jesus." Will Jesus refuse such a request today? _____
4. JESUS' TESTIMONY (12:23-36a).
Compare Jesus' words "The hour is come" (12:23) with
the multitudes' earlier exclamation "Blessed is the King of
Israel that cometh" (12:13). What did the multitudes

want? _____

What was Jesus ready to offer? _____
This passage contains many wonderful statements by
Jesus. Make a list of these, and of the truths that can be
applied to your own life.

III. NOTES.

1. "And not for that nation only" (11:52). Jesus died for
Gentiles as well as for Jews.
2. "Spikenard" (12:3). This was an expensive ointment
imported from northern India.
3. "Hosanna" (12:13). Literally, this Hebrew term means
"Save, I pray" (cf. Ps. 118:25-26). On the occasion of
Jesus' entry into Jerusalem it was more an ascription of
praise.
4. "Life" (12:25). Two Greek words are translated "life"
in this verse. The verse may be paraphrased thus: "He who
loves his *psuche* (life in the physical body) shall lose it,
but he who puts his *psuche* second in importance in this
world shall guard it to *zoe* (spiritual life) eternal."
5. "Father, save me from this hour" (12:27). If this was
a prayer of Jesus, it anticipates the agony which He later

experienced in Gethsemane (cf. Matt. 26:38-42). Some versions translate the words as a question, thus: "Shall I say, 'Father, do not let this hour come upon me'? But that is why I came, to go through this hour of suffering" (TEV).

IV. FURTHER ADVANCED STUDY.

Think more about the significances of the Lazarus miracle. How was such a miracle a combination of many miracles?

_____

Can miracles be fully described in human language, even in the words of Scripture? _____

The raising of Lazarus is the last miracle recorded by John in the main body of his gospel. (The resurrection and postresurrection appearances of Jesus stand in a category by themselves, and the draught of fishes is part of the epilogue.) You might want to make a comparative study of the miracles of John's gospel. Look for such things as the need bringing on the miracle, the method used by Jesus, attributes of Jesus revealed, and effects on the people and disciples.

Recall from 20:30-31 what John's main purpose was in reporting these miracles. Were Jesus' purposes, in performing them, the same as John's, in reporting them? _____

_____

V. SOME APPLICATIONS.

1. What do you learn from:

a. Jesus' love for Lazarus _____

b. Mary's love for Jesus _____

c. Judas' cold heart _____

d. The people's praise of Jesus (12:12-15) _____

2. What kind of service does Jesus expect of His disciples (12:25-26)? _____

_____

3. What are the most important lessons you have learned from your study of this lesson? _____

_____

VI. WORDS TO PONDER.

"Jesus wept" (11:35).

* * *

VII. SUMMARY OF 5:1—12:36a.

The section 5:1—12:36a covers about two years of Jesus' public ministry, which were marked by a growing hate of the Jewish rulers against Jesus because of His claims to Messiahship and divine sonship. These religionists had one goal: kill Jesus.

Many of the multitudes gave a sympathetic ear to Jesus' claims, and demonstrated their support by giving Him a royal reception as He rode into Jerusalem on an ass. There were not a few of these who believed on Him.

And then there were Jesus' close friends and disciples. For the most part they are in the background in John's gospel during these chapters, but all references to them reveal a loyal group of followers (Judas was the exception).

Throughout this period of conflict with His enemies, Jesus faithfully performed His mission. He told who He was, He demonstrated who He was, and He invited all people to believe on Him to be saved. When that mission was over, He "walked no more openly among the Jews" (11:54), for He was ready now to accomplish a more private ministry to the twelve disciples. This is the subject of the next main section of John's gospel.

DAY OF PREPARATION
Events Attending the Last Supper

AT THIS POINT IN HIS GOSPEL JOHN

BEGINS TO CONCENTRATE ON JESUS'

PRIVATE MINISTRY TO HIS DISCIPLES.

In 12:12-19 John had reported Jesus' triumphal entry into Jerusalem, which took place on Sunday of Passion Week. The passage 12:20-36a could be dated on Tuesday of that week, and the words, "Jesus . . . departed, and did hide himself" (12:36b), could refer to Wednesday, about which all four gospel writers are silent. All of Jesus' discourses to His disciples reported only by John (chaps. 13—17) were spoken on Thursday, around the occasion of the Last Supper.

Sayings of Jesus reported in the first half of John's gospel were mainly directed to unbelievers, for those were years of conflict with His opposition. The discourses reported in this new section of John (chaps. 13—17) are mainly for believers, for these were blessed truths which Jesus spoke to and about His disciples.

I. PREPARATION FOR STUDY.

1. Refer to Chart D and renew your survey acquaintance with John's gospel. Observe how these lines describe the entire section 12:36b—17:26:

> Private Ministry
> Self Revealed
> Day of Preparation
> Ministering to His Close Disciples

2. Study Chart P, which identifies Jesus' activities in Passion Week. Locate the passage of our present lesson on the chart.

KING
EXTOLLED

KING
MOCKED

Ministry to Public (Luke 21:37-38)			Ministry to Disciples		Solitary Ministry
Sunday	Monday	Tuesday	Wednesday	Thursday	Friday
Active Days			Quiet Days		Violent Day
Authority			Compassion		Submission
Jesus	speaks	much			Jesus speaks little

Marching
into the city
on a colt
(John 12:12-19)

Driven
out of the city
bearing a cross
(John 19:17)

II. ANALYSIS.

Segments to be analyzed: 12:36b-50; also 13:1-38.
Paragraph divisions: at verses 12:36b; 44; also 13:1, 12, 18, 31, 36.

A. Transitional Segment (12:36b-50).

Think of these transitional verses as functioning in the structure of John's gospel as shown on Chart Q.

1. Read 12:37-43. This paragraph is really a parenthesis between 12:36 and 12:44. Observe John's three comments on the people's unbelief:

    a. It was not logical (12:37).
    b. It had been foretold (12:38).
    c. It was a result of hardness of heart (12:39-40).

Concerning the last verses, does God keep a person from believing? _____

Read Matthew 13:14-15 for light on this quote from Isaiah 6.

FUNCTION OF TRANSITIONAL VERSES

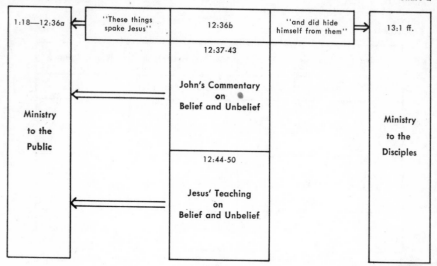

2. Read 12:44-50. What does Jesus teach about belief and unbelief here? _____

_____

B. Discourses at the Last Supper (13:1-38).

Read these paragraphs carefully and prayerfully. Try to visualize the scenes, and sense the tone of Jesus' words. What are your first impressions after reading this chapter?

_____

How is verse 1 an introduction to the theme of the entire chapter? _____

What was Jesus mainly teaching in His washing of the disciples' feet? _____

How often does Judas appear in the story? What do you think is meant by the phrase "Satan entered into him" (13:27)? _____

_____

What does this chapter teach about the following subjects:

Christian Love and Fellowship _____

Humility _____

Service _____

Discipleship _____

Loyalty _____

Self-confidence _____

Defection _____

III. NOTES.

1. "Before the feast of the passover" (13:1). Some take this to mean that the supper of verse 2 was not a Passover meal (Thursday) but a preparatory fellowship meal. For an able defense of the position that it was a Passover meal, see A. T. Robertson, *A Harmony of the Gospels,* pages 279-84. The phrase "supper being ended" is translated in some versions as "during supper" (e.g., ASV).

2. "Dipped the sop" (13:26). This was a custom whereby a morsel of bread was dipped in sauce and extended to the person as a token of friendship. What does Jesus' gesture reveal about His heart of love?

3. "It was night" (13:30). Everett F. Harrison writes of this,

> In a writing so sensitive to symbolism and underlying meaning as this Gospel, these words must have special significance. They picture at once the benighted condition of Judas through surrender to hatred of Jesus and also the coming of the hour when the powers of darkness would engulf the Saviour.*

4. "A new commandment" (13:34). This was new because of the disciples' new relationship to God through Jesus Christ (hence Jesus' words, "as I have loved you").

IV. FURTHER ADVANCED STUDY.

Some Christians hold that foot-washing is an ordinance for the church as well as an example given by Christ. Make a study of the Bible passages on this subject.

* Charles F. Pfeiffer and Everett F. Harrison (eds.), *The Wycliffe Bible Commentary,* p. 1103.

Study all the Bible references to Judas, Jesus' betrayer. Include Psalm 41:9 in your research.

V. APPLICATIONS.

Picture yourself as one of Jesus' disciples listening to Him at this Last Supper. What would have struck home at your heart, of the things He said in this passage?

VI. WORDS TO PONDER.

"This is how all men will know that you are my disciples, because you have such love for one another" (John 13:35, Phillips).

Farewell Discourses

ANYONE WHO ASKS THE QUESTION,

'WHAT KIND OF A PERSON WAS JESUS?'

WILL FIND A THOUSAND ANSWERS IN JOHN.

This is particularly true in the section 12:36*b*—17:26. The three chapters of our present lesson contain three farewell discourses of Jesus delivered to His disciples on the evening before His crucifixion. The first discourse, chapter 14, was probably spoken in the upper room where the last supper (chap. 13) was held.* The last phrase of 14:31 suggests that Jesus and His disciples left the house and started walking east toward the Garden of Gethsemane. The second discourse (15:1—16:4*a*) and the third (16:4*b*-33) may then have been spoken as the group moved quietly through the city.† The high-priestly prayer of chapter 17 was prayed before Jesus and His disciples crossed the Kidron Valley on their way to Gethsemane.

I. PREPARATION FOR STUDY.

One cannot read these long discourses and prayer of Jesus without recognizing the supernatural inspiration which was given John the author to know what to record. As you study these chapters, open your heart to this wonderful divine revelation. Thank God for giving you this Word. And determine in your heart that you will be a better Christian as a fruit of your study.

The three farewell discourses could be called one discourse, because they are so intimately related. For purposes of study, however, it is helpful to recognize three

---

* Some Bible students prefer to regard 13:31-38 as part of this first discourse. The content is not affected either way.

† It is difficult to say where the second discourse ends and the third begins because of the constantly recurring subjects which Jesus spoke about in this informal conversation with His disciples.

separate units, and analyze these accordingly. The main subjects of the discourses may be identified thus:

FIRST DISCOURSE	SECOND DISCOURSE	THIRD DISCOURSE
14:1 14:31 The Father's House	15:1 16:4a Vine and the Branches	16:4b 16:33 Promises of Jesus

II. ANALYSIS.

Segments to be analyzed: 14:1-31; 15:1—16:4a; 16:4b-33. *Paragraph divisions*: at verses 14:1, 8, 12, 15, 27; 15:1, 12, 18; 16:4b, 16, 25.

A limited number of suggestions as to what to look for in these chapters are given below. You will want to extend your studies beyond these exercises. Because of the informal setting of Jesus' discourses, with occasional interruptions by some of His disciples, no clear-cut outline can be determined for many parts of the discourses. The outlines suggested below will give some direction for study; you should try arriving at your own outlines after you have familiarized yourself with the text.

A. First Discourse: The Father's House (14:1-31).

1. INTRODUCTION (14:1).
How does the opening phrase introduce the subject of peace? _____

_____

Compare this with verse 27, which begins the conclusion of the discourse.

2. COMING TO THE FATHER BY BELIEVING JESUS (14:2-7).
Observe the key phrase "cometh unto the Father" (14:6).
What aspect of salvation is taught by this phrase? _____

_____

What does verse 6 teach about the way of salvation? _____

_____

3. KNOWING THE FATHER THROUGH KNOWING JESUS (14:8-11).

What do these verses teach about knowing the Father? ___

4. WORKING FOR THE FATHER THROUGH JESUS' WORKING (14:12-14).

What do works have to do with the Christian life? _____

5. LOVED BY THE FATHER THROUGH LOVING JESUS (14:15-26).

What verse contains the phrase "loved of my Father"? What are the rewards for loving Jesus and His Father?

_____

6. CONCLUSION (14:27-31).

Relate verse 27 to verse 1. How was such a promise of peace important in view of the statement "the prince of

this world cometh" (14:30)? _____

_____

Who is this prince? _____
How is the rest of the paragraph a summary of the dis-

course? _____
Write a list of the prominent truths taught in this first discourse about the Son; the Father; and the Holy Spirit.

_____

What are the commands to believers, and promises? Look for these same truths as they are taught in the next two

discourses. _____

_____

B. Second Discourse: Vine and the Branches (15:1—16:4a).

1. RELATIONSHIP OF BELIEVERS TO JESUS (15:1-11).
How intimate is the relationship of the believer to Jesus, according to the figure of vine and branch? _____

_____

What are the key words of this paragraph? _____

_____

What is the prominent command? _____

_____

What is the promised blessing? _____

_____

What is meant by the severe judgment cited in verse 6?

_____

What is suggested by the word "much" in the phrase "much fruit"? _____

2. RELATIONSHIP OF BELIEVERS TO EACH OTHER (15:12-17).

What is the basic command here? _____

_____

What are some of the things Jesus meant when He said, "As I have loved you" (v. 12)? _____

_____

3. RELATIONSHIP OF BELIEVERS TO THE WORLD (15:18—16:4a).
What main state of affairs does Jesus recognize in verses 18-25? _____

How is 15:26—16:4a related to this? _____

_____

What help can Christians depend on in times of persecution? _____

C. Third Discourse: Promises of Jesus (16:4b-33).

As you read this discourse, think of the many ways in which Jesus gave comfort and inspiration to His disciples at this critical hour. The following outline suggests one line of thought for your study.

1. PROMISE OF GUIDANCE (16:4b-15).

Who of the Trinity is especially designated as the Christian's Teacher and Comforter today? _____

Is it the function of the Spirit to glorify the Son, or the Son to glorify the Spirit (v. 14)? _____

Why is the knowledge of truth (v. 13) so necessary for successful living? _____

_____

2. PROMISE OF JOY (16:16-24).

What is taught here about joy after sorrow? _____

_____

About prayer? _____

3. PROMISE OF VICTORY (16:25-33).

What is taught here about victory through tribulation?

_____

How significant were the words of verse 33 on the lips of Jesus in view of His approaching trial and crucifixion?

_____

III. NOTES.

1. "Greater works" (14:12). The comparison concerns scope, and suggests how extensive the ministry of the gospel would become.

2. "Comforter" (14:16). The Greek *parakletos* ("one called to the side of") may be translated "helper."

3. "A little while, and ye shall not see me" (16:16). This is a reference to Jesus' death. The next part of the verse refers to His postresurrection appearances.

4. "Proverbs" (16:25). The reference is to obscure sayings. The truths about Jesus' death and resurrection and other

vital doctrines were obscure to the disciples at this time because these were not the kinds of events the disciples were expecting.

IV. FURTHER ADVANCED STUDY.

Here are some suggested areas of study, related to this lesson:
1. the Holy Spirit and His relation to the Trinity
2. the kind of love which Christians should be demonstrating
3. effective prayer
4. what it means to abide in Christ

V. APPLICATIONS.

These chapters are filled with vital spiritual lessons for Christian living today. Make a list of ten such lessons, and compare your list with those of other members of your group.

VI. WORDS TO PONDER.

"In the world ye shall have tribulation: but be of good cheer; I have overcome the world" (16:33).

High-priestly Prayer

JESUS' HIGH-PRIESTLY PRAYER IN JOHN 17

HAS BEEN CALLED THE NEW TESTAMENT'S

NOBLEST AND PUREST PEARL OF DEVOTION.

When John Knox was dying he whispered to his wife, "Go, read where I first cast my anchor." And without further instruction she turned to John 17.

A Christian cannot read this chapter without being warmed in heart over the tremendous fact that his Lord prays to the Father on *his* behalf.

We would like to be able to reconstruct the setting of this five-minute prayer of Jesus, but no details are given in the account, other than that Jesus lifted up His eyes to heaven (17:1), and spoke the words in the presence of the eleven disciples (cf. 18:1). Few details, but an awesome truth: the Son of God speaking to His Father in heaven about His disciples!

I. PREPARATION FOR STUDY.

As you approach this chapter, think of the heart needs of the disciples at this time. Also, think how Jesus was feeling at this time, knowing what trying experiences were awaiting Him in the next hours.

Before you begin to analyze the prayer for what it teaches, enter into its atmosphere by reading it aloud, slowly and softly, in one sitting. Read it in the manner you think Jesus may have uttered it at the time. Such interpretative reading can be a very illuminating experience.

II. ANALYSIS.

Segment to be analyzed: 17:1-26.
Paragraph divisions: at verses 1, 6, 20.

The prayer is clearly of three main parts. Chart **R** gives an outline around which you may organize your study. Use this work sheet to record key words and phrases, and to show relations between parts.

JESUS PRAYS
17:1-26

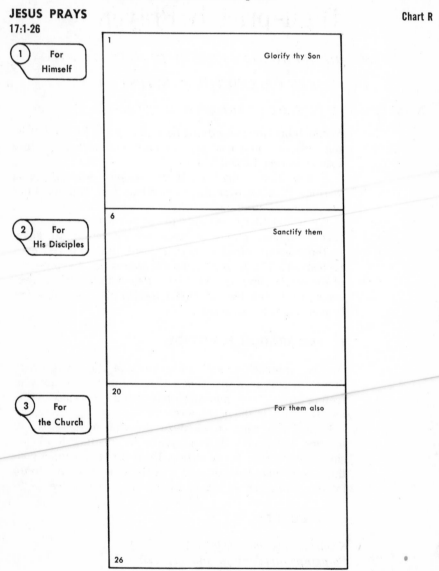

1   For
    Himself

1
Glorify thy Son

2   For
    His Disciples

6
Sanctify them

3   For
    the Church

20
For them also

26

1. Read 17:1-5. What is the basic petition of verse 1? _____

What various truths are taught about Christ's glory in this paragraph? _____

What is eternal life, according to these verses? _____ _____

2. Read 17:6-19. Who are "the men which thou gavest me" (17:6)? _____

What does Jesus say about these men in this paragraph? _____

Study the context and meaning of the two petitions, "Keep [them]" (v. 11) and "Sanctify them" (v. 17). Compare the phrases "for the world" (v. 9); "in the world" (v. 11); "of the world" (v. 14); "out of the world" (v. 15); "into

the world" (v. 18). _____ . _____

3. Read 17:20-26. For whom is Jesus praying here? What

are His petitions? _____ _____

What is taught here about "love" and "glory"? _____ _____

As you think back over this prayer of Jesus, what are some of the great blessings associated with Christ's gift of eternal

life? _____ _____

III. NOTES.

1. "I pray not for the world" (17:9). This does not reflect a disinterest on the part of Jesus toward unsaved people. He can only pray the prayer of John 17 for those who choose to come to God by Him.

2. "The son of perdition" (17:12). Judas was lost. "Jesus was saying that the loss was not a reflection on His keeping

power as the shepherd of the flock. Rather, Judas had never really belonged to him except in a nominal, external sense (cf. 13:10-11)."*

IV. FURTHER ADVANCED STUDY.

Study what the Bible teaches about
1. sanctification
2. common fellowship of believers
   A concordance, topical handbook, and a book on doctrines will be of help for such studies.

V. APPLICATIONS.

Read this high-priestly prayer again, and whenever reference is made to a believer, read your name instead (if you are a believer). This may prove to be your most enjoyable moment in this study.

VI. WORDS TO PONDER.

"I do not ask you to take them out of the world, but I do ask you to keep them safe from the Evil One" (17:15, TEV).

---

* *The Wycliffe Bible Commentary,* p. 1112.

HOUR OF SACRIFICE
Arrested and Tried

JESUS HAD NO SLEEP THURSDAY NIGHT,

FOR THE DIVINELY PROGRAMMED FINAL

COUNTDOWN FOR HIS CRUCIFIXION HAD BEGUN.

After the high-priestly prayer of chapter 17 the succession of events was this:

    Soul-Agony of Gethsemane*
    Arrest
    Trials
    Scourging
    Crucifixion
    Death

Not one of these experiences did Jesus try to delay, or avoid. To the very end, His attitude was one of obedience to His Father's will: "The cup which my Father hath given me, shall I not drink it?" (18:11; cf. Matt. 26:1-2). In your study of John's account you will observe that even some of the *details* of these last events had been prophesied hundreds of years earlier in the Old Testament Scriptures. That Jesus was not a fatalist concerning such a sovereignly fixed program is shown throughout the Gospels by the intensity of His human emotions in the midst of each trying experience. This Man of sorrows, acquainted with grief, was "obedient unto death, even the death of the cross" (Phil. 2:8).

I. PREPARATION FOR STUDY.

1. As background for 18:1-11, read the Gethsemane account as given in Matthew 26:30, 36-46 (cf. Mark 14:26, 32-42; Luke 22:39-46).

* John makes only the brief mention of Jesus entering the Garden of Gethsemane with His disciples (18:1).

2. Keep in mind that Jesus was confronted by two different realms of authority in His trial. The political rulers were Roman, and the religious rulers were Jewish. Shown below are the two confrontations, with three stages in each. Note how much is reported by John.

Jewish Trial
1. Before Annas (John 18:12-14, 19-23).
2. Informal trial by Sanhedrin before dawn (John 18:24; Matt. 26:57, 59-68; Mark 14:53, 55-65; Luke 22:54, 63-65).
3. Formal trial after dawn (Matt. 27:1; Mark 15:1; Luke 22:66-71).

Roman Trial
1. First appearance before Pilate (John 18:28-38; Matt. 27:2, 11-14; Mark 15:1-5; Luke 23:1-5).
2. Before Herod Antipas (Luke 23:6-12).
3. Final appearance before Pilate (John 18:39—19:16a; Matt. 27:15-26; Mark 15:6-15; Luke 23:13-25).

II. ANALYSIS.

Segment to be analyzed: 18:1—19:16a.
Paragraph divisions: at verses 18:1, 12, 15, 19, 25, 28, 33, 38b; 19:1, 12.
As you read this passage, try to catch the tone and feeling of each part. This will reveal much of the significant truths involved. Here are two topical studies to pursue for the passage:

A. Observe and Record.
1. words directed to Jesus
2. words spoken by Jesus

In each case, try to determine what was meant, what brought on the words, and what effect the words had.

B. Comparative Study.
For 18:28—19:16a, make a comparative study of Pilate's estimate of Jesus, and the Jews' estimate of Jesus. The following study questions will lead you into other important subjects of this passage.
1. Read 18:1-11. Who takes the initiative in this scene? Observe Jesus' tender concern for His disciples (v. 8).

2. Read 18:12-14, 19-24. The high priest of verse 19 is Annas. Translate verse 24 thus: "So Annas sent him bound unto Caiaphas the high priest." Observe that Jesus insisted that He always told the truth.

3. Read 18:16-18, 25-27 (cf. 13:38). What important lesson do you learn from these denials by Peter? _____

4. Read 18:28-32. What was Pilate's wish? On verse 31b, see Notes. For verse 32, compare Matthew 20:19. _____

5. Read 18:33—19:16a. Meditate long over the truths suggested by these powerful phrases:

    Art thou a king? (18:37).
    What is truth? (18:38).
    I find no fault in him (18:38).
    Behold the man! (19:5).
    Crucify him! (19:6).
    We have no king but Caesar (19:15).

III. NOTES.

1. "Annas" (18:13). Caiaphas was the official high priest; Annas his father-in-law had been the official high priest earlier (A.D. 6-15), and was now serving with his son-in-law in an unofficial capacity. (Cf. Luke 3:2; Acts 4:5-6.)

2. "Another disciple" (18:15). This may have been the Apostle John.

3. "Hall of judgment" (18:28). This was Governor Pilate's headquarters.

4. "It is not lawful for us to put any man to death" (18:31). On occasion the Jews were permitted to stone a person who had violated the temple precincts. According to Roman law, however, only the Roman authorities had the power of execution, and this was by crucifixion.

5. "Scourged him" (19:1). This was cruel torture by beating, using rods or weighted whips. Most victims fainted; many died (read Isa. 53:5).

IV. FURTHER ADVANCED STUDY.

1. Study the subject of Jesus and the kingdom, using outside helps.

2. Study the symbolic meanings of some of the parts of this narrative, such as "passover," "king," "crown," "thorns" (see Gen. 3:17-18).

V. APPLICATIONS.

What does this story of Jesus have to do with today? For example, are people today crying out, in essence, "We have no king but Caesar"? See how much of sinful human nature is revealed in this passage, and make the applications.

VI. WORDS TO PONDER.

"My kingdom is not of this world" (18:36).

Crucified and Buried

DEATH ITSELF IS ALWAYS COLD AND

ABRUPT, MOVING IN AS A DARK CLOUD

TO DO ITS WORK OF SEPARATION.

The story of Jesus' death should never be glamorized. The redemptive fruits of Christ's death are glorious, but the hour of His death was mankind's darkest hour. Even nature itself echoed this, with the darkening of the sun and the violent earthquake (Luke 23:45; Matt. 27:51).

If Jesus did not die physically, then He really did not die.

If all the sins of mankind were not placed on Jesus in His death, then He did not die for all men's sins.

If Jesus did not really suffer on the cross, then judgment for sin is a light matter.

If Jesus did not die, then He did not finish the Father's work.

If Jesus did not really die, the Bible is a lie.

But Jesus did die, as John so clearly reports, "They . . . saw that he was dead" (19:33). How He died, and what His friends did with His body, is the story of this lesson.

I. PREPARATION FOR STUDY.

The Gospels give no detailed description of the process of Roman crucifixion. The text usually reads only briefly, as in John, "They crucified him." Can you suggest a reason for this relative silence? Consult a Bible dictionary for a full description of crucifixion as a Roman form of execution. Also, read Psalm 22:1-21 for a description of some of the physical, mental and spiritual agonies of Jesus on the cross. Consult the dictionary also about the burial customs of Jesus' day.

II. ANALYSIS.

Segment to be analyzed: 19:16b-42.
Paragraph divisions: at verses 16b, 23, 25, 28, 31, 38.

John's account of Jesus' death is brief but weighty. He paints six portraits for us to examine and meditate upon. As you look at these, record your impressions.

Jesus' identity recognized (19:16b-22) _____

_____

_____

Jesus' goods confiscated (19:23-24) _____

_____

_____

Jesus' mother cared for (19:25-27) _____

_____

_____

Jesus' life given (19:28-30) _____

_____

_____

Jesus' death verified (19:31-37) _____

_____

_____

Jesus' body buried (19:38-42) _____

_____

_____

1. Read these prophecies which were fulfilled at this time: Psalm 22:18; 34:20; Zechariah 12:10.

2. Which paragraphs record words of Jesus? _____
How would you compare Jesus' thoughts in each paragraph? _____

3. What symbolic teaching is suggested by the blood and by the water which flowed from Jesus' side (19:34)? _____

_____

4. How significant is it that Nicodemus was one of the men who claimed Jesus' body to prepare it for burial? _____

_____

III. NOTES.

1. "His mother's sister" (19:25). Probably Salome, mother of John.
2. "I thirst" (19:28). This was a cry of physical anguish, not an appeal for its alleviation.
3. "That their legs might be broken" (19:31). The breaking of the victim's legs was intended to hasten his death.

IV. FURTHER ADVANCED STUDY.

Jesus' words "It is finished" (19:30) are significant with respect to the doctrine of salvation. Refer to the epistle to the Hebrews to learn what is said there about the finality of Christ's death (e.g., Heb. 9:23-28).

V. APPLICATIONS.

What does the death of Jesus mean to you? _____

How is your salvation based on it? _____
What did Paul mean when he wrote, "I am crucified with

Christ"? _____
What are some of the manifestations of such an attitude

in Christian living? _____

VI. WORDS TO PONDER.

"And he bowed his head, and gave up the ghost" (19:30).

DAWN OF VICTORY
Signs of the Resurrected Jesus

THE RESURRECTION OF JESUS WAS BOTH

PRESCHEDULED OF GOD AND WHOLLY

UNANTICIPATED BY THE DISCIPLES.

Jesus had clearly instructed His disciples earlier about His forthcoming death and resurrection (Mark 8:31-32), but they did not understand the meaning then, nor did they even remember the words later. Understanding would come of believing, and believing would come through signs. John 20 records for us some of the signs which restored the disciples of Jesus to a personal and new relationship to Him as the risen Lord. How utter defeat can suddenly and miraculously turn to victory is one of the glowing truths of this chapter.

I. PREPARATION FOR STUDY.

1. Recall the burial procedure of 19:40, including the anointing with spices. Refer to a Bible dictionary for a description of the burial customs of Jesus' day. Mary Magdalene (and other women, Mark 16:1) came to the tomb early Sunday morning to anoint the body of Jesus more permanently (Mark 16:1).

2. Visualize yourself as being one of Jesus' friends or disciples who saw His body committed to the sepulcher. What would you be thinking, now that your Leader was dead, whose prophecies of resurrection you have forgotten?

II. ANALYSIS.

Segment to be analyzed: 20:1-31.
Paragraph divisions: at verses 1, 11, 19, 24, 30.

Read the chapter once or twice with the cited paragraph divisions in mind, making preliminary notations in your Bible. What are your first impressions of the chapter?

How does the phrase "And many other signs" (v. 30) relate to the paragraphs preceding it? _____

What is the chapter's main point? _____

Chart S is a work sheet for recording observations and outlines. Below are suggested some subjects for study. Record all your findings.

1. To whom are signs (miracles with a message) given in each paragraph? (Note the answers already recorded on Chart S as an example of recording observations.) _____

2. What is the particular sign or evidence in each situation?

3. What are the reactions of the people involved? _____

4. Observe every appearance of the word "see" (in its various grammatical forms). How is the word "see" related to the word "signs"? _____

5. How are the phrases "But Mary" (v. 11) and "But Thomas" (v. 24) related to the paragraphs preceding them?

6. What is one major difference between the sign of the first paragraph and the signs of the next three paragraphs?

7. Analyze carefully 20:1-10. Focus your study on the three different Greek verbs translated "saw," "seeth" and "saw," shown on the chart. There is a progression of intensity in the verbs:*

* See Irving L. Jensen, *Independent Bible Study*, pp. 18-19.

SIGNS OF THE RESURRECTED JESUS

20:1-31

SIGNS or PERSONS'
EVIDENCES REACTIONS

To Peter
and John

—apprehensive

1

other disciple . . . SAW (*blepei*) the linen clothes

Simon Peter . . . SEETH (*theorei*)

other disciple . . . SAW (*eiden*)

To Mary

—weeping

11

BUT MARY stood without

To the
Disciples

—intimidated

19

To Thomas

—doubting

24

BUT THOMAS . . . was not with them

30

Many other signs . . . .

31

John: *blepei*: this is mere partial *viewing* of the burial spot from the entrance to the tomb, apparently without any significant reaction other than the affirmation that what Mary had reported was true.

Peter: *theorei*: this is *beholding* something astounding. Peter saw, closeup, the napkin, or head roll, all rolled up, still intact like a cocoon.

John: *eiden*: this is *perceiving* to the point of belief. John perceived that here was something impossible, and God had done it. So he believed.

Reconstruct the action of the paragraph with the above meanings in mind.

8. Extend this study of the verb "see" to the remainder of the chapter, according to these translations: the "seeth" (v. 12) and "saw" (v. 14) are *theorei*; and the "seen" (v. 18), "saw" (v. 20), "seen," and "see" (v. 25) are from the root *eiden*.

9. Read 20:11-18. Explain why Mary recognized Jesus when he said "Mary," whereas she didn't recognize Him when He first spoke (v. 15). _____

_____

10. Read 20:19-23. Account for the disciples' fear of the Jews (v. 19). _____

What different message is introduced by each appearance of the blessing "Peace be unto you"? _____

_____

11. Read 20:24-29. Whose word was unconvincing to Thomas? _____

What is significant about each part of the affirmation "My Lord and my God"? _____

12. Study the content of Jesus' doctrinal teaching at the end of the second, third and fourth paragraphs. Record what you think is being taught in each case:

20:17 _____

20:21-23 _____

20:29 _____

13. Analyze the key verses 20:30-31. Record all the truths

taught by these verses. Then compare your findings with this outline:†

> Selective Gospel: "many other . . . but these"
> Attested Gospel: "in the presence of his disciples"
> Apologetic Gospel: "these are written, that ye might"
> Interpretative Gospel: "that Jesus is the Christ"
> Definitive Gospel: "the Son of God"
> Effective Gospel: "ye might have life"

III. NOTES.

1. "Wrapped together" (20:7). The Greek word suggests a winding of the graveclothes around Jesus' body in the form of a cocoon.
2. "Touch me not" (20:17). The strength of the Greek is "Stop clinging to me." Jesus allowed the touching of His resurrected body at this time (cf. Matt. 28:9; John 20:27), but not the intimate "clinging" of the former relationship before Calvary. Jesus wanted to remind His friends that the new era of His glorification had begun.
3. "Whose soever sins ye remit . . ." (20:23). Jesus intended by these words that the disciples should declare the fact and the how of God's forgiveness of sins.‡

IV. FURTHER ADVANCED STUDY.

What kind of a resurrection body will we as believers have? Study I Corinthians 15 for much light on this. Is Jesus' resurrection body a clue to what ours will be like? _____

V. APPLICATIONS.

1. In what kinds of situations do Christians need the comfort and assurance of Jesus' "Peace be unto you"? _____
2. The phrase "so send I you" (v. 21) is a classic missionary marker.§ Build a list of comparisons of the two parts of the equation, and apply these to present-day Christian service:

† Outline by Merrill C. Tenney, *John: The Gospel of Belief*, pp. 34-36.
‡ Refer to commentaries for extended treatment of this verse.
§ Read the stanzas of the hymn "So Send I You" if you have access to this.

"AS MY FATHER HATH SENT ME"	"EVEN SO SEND I YOU"

VI. WORDS TO PONDER.

"Blessed are they that have not seen, and yet have believed" (20:29).

Postresurrection Appearances in Galilee

IN THE CLOSING CHAPTER OF JOHN WE

READ OF A THIRD APPEARANCE OF JESUS

TO HIS DISCIPLES BY THE SEA OF GALILEE.

The survey Chart D shows chapter 21 as an epilogue, suggesting a formal conclusion of the gospel with the verses 20:30-31. In another sense, however, chapter 21 is not detached from chapter 20, because John here reports more evidence of the miracle of Christ's resurrection. (To sense this natural continuity, try reading 21:1 immediately after 20:29.) *

I. PREPARATION FOR STUDY.

Try to imagine what constituted the disciples' daily life from the day Jesus first appeared to them in His resurrection body until He ascended into heaven (Acts 1:9). Did they have any explicit instructions for living, from Jesus? What do you imagine they were thinking about and discussing as they met together from time to time? What was their source of income for the physical needs of life? What may have been their plans for the future? Ponder these things as you prepare to study John 21.

II. ANALYSIS.

Segment to be analyzed: 21:1-25.
Paragraph divisions: at verses 1, 15, 20, 24.
There are three main paragraphs in this chapter, followed by the concluding verses 24-25. Study the paragraphs carefully, and record your observations on paper. Begin by

---

° Perhaps a better reconstruction of the organizational structure of the last two chapters of John is done not in explaining why chapter 21 was added to chapter 20, but in explaining why John placed 20:30-31 at the end of chapter 20 rather than at the close of the entire gospel.

identifying the main characters besides Jesus in each paragraph.

A. Miracle (21:1-14).

Why was Jesus not recognized as He stood on the shore (v. 4)? _____

What brought recognition later (v. 7)? _____

_____

What truths did the disciples learn from this appearance of Jesus which supplemented what they had learned in the first two appearances (chap. 20)? _____

_____

B. Challenge (21:15-19).

What was the main question which Jesus asked Peter? ____

_____

Relate this to the invitation given Peter at the end of the conversation (v. 19). _____

You may want to make a comparative study of the various words spoken in this two-way conversation. The words are listed below.

	Jesus' Question	Peter's Answer	Jesus' Response
Verse 15	Lovest? (agapas)†	I love (filo)	Feed my lambs
Verse 16	Lovest? (agapas)	I love (filo)	Shepherd my sheep‡
Verse 17	Lovest? (fileis)	I love (filo)	Shepherd my sheep

Do you think there was a connection between Jesus' thrice-repeated question and Peter's earlier threefold denial?

† The Greek word *agapas* in this context has the meaning of unselfish love, ready to serve. The *filo* of Peter's answer suggests intimate and tender affection. See W. E. Vine, *An Expository Dictionary of New Testament Words*, III, 20-22.
‡ The Greek word of v. 16 is different from the one translated "feed" in v. 15.

C. Correction (21:20-23).

Who is the one being corrected here? _____

For what did Jesus correct him? _____

D. Conclusion (21:24-25).

Note the "we" of verse 24 and the "I" of verse 25. Verse 24 may have been written by close associates of John, such as elders of the church at Ephesus.

Compare verse 25 with 20:30-31. Is it natural to interpret that John was author of both concluding statements?

III. NOTES.

1. "I go a fishing" (21:3). Of this, Everett F. Harrison writes, "It is hazardous to conclude that Peter was going back to fishing as a permanent occupation."§
2. "Another shall gird thee" (21:18). This may be translated "another shall fasten them," referring to the hands being fastened to the cross. The phrase "thou shalt stretch forth thy hands" (v. 18) is a reference to the crucifixion form of execution.

IV. FURTHER ADVANCED STUDY.

The appearance of the two different Greek words for "love" in this passage suggests a topical study of *love* which would be an appropriate conclusion to your work in the gospel of John. An exhaustive concordance and books on word studies will be of much help here. As you think back over the gospel of John, how prominent was the subject of *love* on Jesus' lips as He spoke to His disciples?

V. APPLICATIONS.

We can learn at least two vital lessons about Christian discipleship and service from this final chapter of John. One is that our love for Christ is a basic condition for fruitful service (21:15-19). The other is that Christ holds

§ *The Wycliffe Bible Commentary*, p. 1121. In this commentary Harrison gives reasons for this interpretation.

106

us responsible for the performance of our own service, not service by others (21:20-23).

VI. WORDS TO PONDER.

"Jesus saith unto them, Come and dine" (21:12).

A Review of John

Below are listed some of the major subjects which are part of John's gospel. See how much you can recall of each subject, from your study of this gospel.

About Jesus
Jesus as Incarnate Son; His relation to the Father
His trials
His crucifixion and resurrection

Some Doctrines
Way of salvation
Eternal life
The Holy Spirit

Various Subjects
Miracles as signs
Opposition by the Jews
Training of the twelve
Purpose of John's gospel (20:30-31)

Practical Subjects
Belief and unbelief
Witnessing
Christian love
Prayer
Attaining wisdom

*   *   *

"Jesus did many other mighty works in his disciples' presence which are not written down in this book. These have been written that you may believe that Jesus is the Messiah, the Son of God, and that through this faith *you may have life in his name*" (20:30-31, TEV).

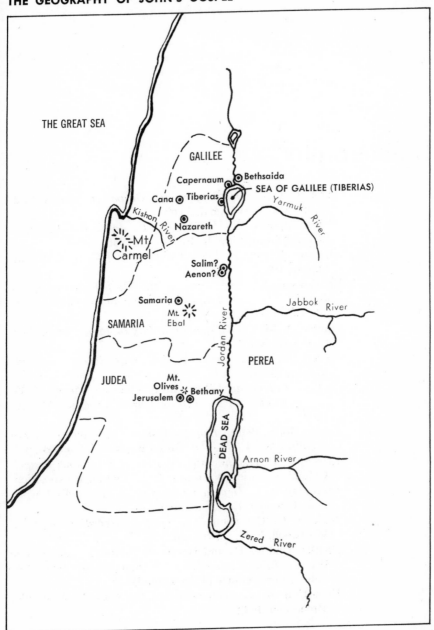

THE GREAT SEA

GALILEE

Capernaum ⊙ Bethsaida

Cana ⊙ Tiberias ⊙ SEA OF GALILEE (TIBERIAS)

Kishon River Yarmuk River

Nazareth

Mt. Carmel

Salim?
Aenon? ⊙

Samaria ⊙ Jabbok River
Mt. Ebal

SAMARIA

Jordan River

PEREA

JUDEA Mt. Olives Bethany

Jerusalem ⊙⊙

DEAD SEA

Arnon River

Zered River

Bibliography

Godet, F. L. *Commentary on the Gospel of John.* Grand Rapids: Zondervan, n.d. 2 vols.

Griffith-Thomas, W. H. *The Apostle John: His Life and Writing.* Grand Rapids: Eerdmans, 1946.

Harrison, Everett F. *John, The Gospel of Faith.* Chicago: Moody, 1968.

Hendriksen, W. *Exposition of the Gospel According to John* in *The New Testament Commentary.* Grand Rapids: Baker, 1953. 2 vols.

Hunter, A. M. *The Gospel According to John.* Cambridge: U. Press, 1965.

Jensen, Irving L. *Acts: An Inductive Study.* Chicago: Moody, 1968.

_____. *Independent Bible Study.* Chicago: Moody, 1963.

_____. *Studies in the Life of Christ.* Chicago: Moody, 1969.

Lange, John Peter. *Lange's Commentary on the Holy Scriptures.* Vol. 17, *John.* Grand Rapids: Zondervan, n.d.

Lenski, R. C. H. *The Interpretation of St. John's Gospel.* Columbus, Ohio: Wartburg, 1942. Thorough exposition.

Macaulay, J. C. *Devotional Studies in St. John's Gospel.* Grand Rapids: Eerdmans, 1945.

Morgan, G. Campbell. *The Gospel According to John.* Westwood, N.J.: Revell, n.d.

Pfeiffer, Charles F., and Harrison, Everett F. (eds.). *The Wycliffe Bible Commentary.* Chicago: Moody, 1962. One-volume commentary of the whole Bible.

Robertson, A. T. *A Harmony of the Gospels.* Nashville: Broadman, 1922.

Scroggie, W. Graham. *St. John: Introduction and Notes.* New York: Harper, 1931. Excellent outlines.

Strong, James. *The Exhaustive Concordance of the Bible.* New York: Abingdon, 1890.

Tenney, Merrill C. *John: The Gospel of Belief.* Grand Rapids: Eerdmans, 1948. Excellent combination of survey and analysis.

_____. *New Testament Survey.* Rev. ed. Grand Rapids: Eerdmans, 1961.

Vine, W. E. *An Expository Dictionary of New Testament Words.* Westwood, N. J.: Revell, 1961.

Westcott, B. F. *The Gospel According to St. John.* Grand Rapids: Eerdmans, 1951. Excellent scholarly treatment.